The *Golf Nut's* Book of Amazing Feats & Records

The
Golf Nut's
Book of
Amazing
Feats &
Records

Bruce Nash
and Allan Zullo
with George White

CB

CONTEMPORARY
BOOKS

CHICAGO

Library of Congress Cataloging-in-Publication Data

Nash, Bruce M.
   The golf nut's book of amazing feats and records
/ Bruce Nash and Allan Zullo ; compiled by George
White.
          p.   cm.
      ISBN 0-8092-3790-3
      1. Golf—Records.   2. Golf—Anecdotes.
I. Zullo, Allan.   II. White, George.   III. Title.
GV967.N38   1994
796.352—dc20   93-42670
                                                          CIP

Cover design and illustration and all interior art by
Mark Anderson

Published by Contemporary Books, Inc.
Two Prudential Plaza, Chicago, Illinois 60601-6790
Manufactured in the United States of America
International Standard Book Number: 0-8092-3790-3
10   9   8   7   6   5   4   3   2   1

To Ron Ziskin, whose creative strokes of genius place him atop the leader board of TV producers.
—Bruce Nash

To Audrae Marzorati, an avid golfer with a habit of standing too close to the ball—after she's hit it.
—Allan Zullo

To my brother Jerry, who's no golfer, but the best sport I know.
—George White

Contents

For the Record

Golf record books are filled with all sorts of statistical information—average putts per green . . . longest driving distance . . . lowest strokes per round.

What do all these records have in common?

They're *boring*!

Unfortunately for golfers, there has never been a record book to capture the wackiest, zaniest, and most bizarre moments of golf. Until now.

As authors of the Sports Hall of Shame book series and creators of the syndicated "Sports Hall of Shame" comic feature, we have chronicled thousands of wild, crazy, and outrageously funny but true stories. In the following pages, we present such little-known nutty golf records as:

- Most golf balls hit to the green while dancing (12, by Fred Astaire)
- Lowest score playing St. Andrews by the light of the moon (93, in 1876)
- Longest time a pro carried an out-of-bounds stake on the Tour (6 months, by Roger Maltbie)
- Highest-priced cow ever won by a pro ($5,000, by Ian Baker-Finch)
- Highest score deliberately taken for a hole in one (3)

With the help of George White, golf writer for the *Orlando Sentinel*, we interviewed pros on the PGA Tour, the LPGA Tour, and the Senior PGA Tour to get the inside scoop on their most offbeat records. We also combed golf publications such as *Golf Digest*, *Golf*, *Golf Week*, and *Golfworld* for backup material, and we received assistance from golf historian Dawson Taylor.

Although many of these records have never been officially documented, we did our best to verify each one. However, we welcome evidence from readers of records that top the ones we included in this book or of new records that we neglected to compile. Flip to the back of the book to learn how to send your contributions to us. We'd love to hear from you.

One thing is certain. The history of this centuries-old sport boasts a rich heritage of hilarious moments from tee to green.

The
Golf Nut's
Book of
Amazing
Feats &
Records

1

Unbelievable Shots

Highest Handicapper to Hit a Double Eagle Off Another Player's Shoe

18-handicapper
Tommy Thomas, 1990
Redstone Golf Course
Redstone Arsenal, Alabama

Tommy Thomas was about to hit his second shot on the par-5, 497-yard third hole at Redstone Golf Course when he noticed the group ahead of him was on the green putting out.

With an 18-handicap, Thomas, of Huntsville, Alabama, had no delusions of reaching the green in two, so he felt totally safe hitting his second shot. Much to his surprise, he caught the ball as solidly as he had ever hit a 3-wood in his life.

As the ball soared straight and true down the fairway, Thomas watched its flight in wonder . . . and then in consternation. He realized that the ball was actually going to reach the green where Ray Stephenson had just knocked in a putt for a birdie.

Oblivious to Thomas's incoming shot, Stephenson happily walked toward the cup to retrieve his ball. Just then, Thomas's ball landed on the green, smacked into the toe of Stephenson's shoe—and ricocheted right into the hole for an incredible double eagle 2!

Out in the fairway, Thomas didn't know whether to hide or celebrate. Rather than be upset over being hit by another golfer's ball, Stephenson was glad to have lent a hand—or in this case a foot—in achieving such a rare feat.

Said Thomas, "It was the best shot I've ever hit in my life."

Longest Distance a Golfer Walked Without Realizing That a Ball Had Been Hit into His Pocket

150 yards
Henry Albert, 1967
Clearview Golf Club
Queens, Long Island, New York

Henry Albert, of Beechurst, New York, was playing the Clearview Golf Club when he felt something lightly brush his slacks. He flicked at it and then hit his approach shot to the fifth hole.

As Albert walked toward the green, a golfer approached him from behind and said, "I hope I didn't hurt you. Would you mind giving my ball back? It was a Wilson Staff."

Albert looked at him in puzzlement. "Well, first off, I'm not aware anybody hit me with a shot. And second, I don't have your Wilson Staff." The other golfer seemed perplexed and walked away.

Albert holed out and then strolled toward the sixth tee, where he reached into his left pocket for a tee—and pulled out a Wilson Staff. "Sure enough, it was the man's golf ball," Albert recalled later. "I didn't own any Wilson Staffs. Then I realized that what I thought was an insect brushing my slacks on the fifth fairway was actually his golf ball entering my pocket." Albert had walked 150 yards with a ball that had been driven into his pocket, and he didn't even know it.

Now Albert was in a quandary. Should he retrace his path back to where the other golfer was playing and tell him the truth? Or should he just ignore the circumstances by which this ball had come into his possession and go on with his round?

Albert opted for the latter. He reasoned that since the golfer had hit his shot earlier than he should have, Albert could have been injured.

So Albert put the Wilson Staff on the tee and swatted it. Fittingly, it promptly disappeared over a fence and out of sight.

Most Yards That a Drive Reversed Direction

250 yards
Mark Witt
1991 Ben Hogan Knoxville Open

Pro golfer Mark Witt hit the longest "boomerang" tee shot in tournament history.

Witt was playing the Ben Hogan Knoxville Open when he smashed a prodigious drive on the par-4, 375-yard 17th hole at Willow Creek Country Club. His tee shot traveled to within 75 yards of the green where it rolled through the fairway and then onto an entrance road to the golf course.

The uphill angle of the road stopped the ball's forward motion and started it rolling back toward the tee. A stunned Witt watched helplessly as the ball slowly headed closer and closer to where he was standing until, after reversing direction for 250 yards, it died just 50 yards from the golfer.

Witt recovered nicely, however. He took a drop from the pavement, then walloped a 3-wood that landed close enough to the green for him to pitch up and make the putt for bogey.

Quickest Payback to an Opponent for Failing to Extend a Common Courtesy

15 seconds
Phil Mickelson
1991 Golf Digest Collegiate Invitational

Phil Mickelson of Arizona State gave his opponent a stunning payback for failing to be a courteous golfer.

Mickelson was matched against Manny Zerman of the University of Arizona at the 1991 Golf Digest Collegiate Invitational. After their tee shots on the final hole at the TPC Woodlands just outside Houston, Mickelson asked Zerman for permission to take a drop out of what he considered casual water. But Zerman refused his opponent's request.

Visibly angered, Mickelson strode to his ball, sized up the 176-yard distance, hooded his 7-iron, and gave it a rip. The ball went screaming toward the flag in a sweeping hook, carrying to the green and then rolling into the hole for a stunning eagle 2 and a dramatic victory.

Mickelson turned and glared at Zerman, who took a breath and replied, "I guess you didn't need that drop after all, did you?"

Lowest Score Made from a Ball Lodged in a Woman's Bosom

3
Gary Player
1968 World Series of Golf

For Gary Player, it was the most unusual par he ever recorded in tournament play.

At the 1968 World Series of Golf, Player was

locked in a tense duel for the lead when he reached the par-3, 178-yard 12th hole at Akron's Firestone Country Club. He hit his tee shot slightly off line to the right, where the green drops off sharply to a stand of cedar trees. The ball appeared headed for real trouble when it flew into the gallery.

Anticipating the worst, Player marched toward the spot where he last saw his ball. When he got there, however, he was surprised to find a woman with her arms folded across her chest, looking very distressed.

Suddenly, Player realized why she looked troubled. There was his ball—lodged between her arms and her breasts. "I didn't know what to do with the ball," the woman told him. "It just bounced into my arms like this and I froze."

This was a problem that required a rules official. If the woman simply unfolded her arms and let the ball drop to the ground, it would have rolled down the slope and into the trees. The official told her to give the ball to Player, who was then allowed to place it at the woman's feet, at a spot only a few yards from the green.

Player then chipped close to the flag and parred the hole.

The woman proved to be extremely critical to the final outcome of the tournament. Had the ball not landed there, Player might well have made bogey or even double bogey. As it was, he went on to win the tournament in a playoff over Bob Goalby.

And who was the woman who saved Player those vital strokes? None other than Mrs. Mark McCormack—the wife of Player's business manager!

Longest Drive Mis-Hit in a PGA Tour Event

787 yards
Carl Cooper
1992 H.E.B. Texas Open

Never before has a tee shot traveled as far as Carl Cooper's odds-defying drive. It went 331 yards *past* the par-4 green!

Cooper, a struggling 31-year-old PGA Tour veteran, gave new meaning to the term *long shot* during the second round of the 1992 H.E.B. Texas Open at San Antonio's Oak Hills Country Club. Using an oversized driver on the 456-yard third hole, Cooper pushed his tee shot way right. The ball carried about 300 yards before heading on a journey that left pros, caddies, officials, and spectators in awe.

After the ball landed on a paved cart path, it followed the asphalt trail by taking one big bounce after another downhill. To everyone's amazement, the ball bounded down the path past the third green . . . then the fifth green . . . beyond the sixth tee . . . all the way to the 12th green!

It might have rolled to Houston had it not finally plunked into a chain link fence. Cooper's caddie measured the stray drive at a whopping 787 yards! That's nearly a half mile—longer than any par-5 and longer than three normal shots of a good player.

"It was just a freak deal," recalled Cooper, who was 190th on the Tour money list. "I wasn't mad or angry that the ball kept going and going. In fact, I was kind of excited that I had hit it so far. Guys who are great players are winning the Masters and the U.S. Open, but nobody has ever hit one this far."

After being given a drop to clear himself from the fence, Cooper needed a 4-iron and an 8-iron just to get back toward the third green. A chip shot and two putts later, he recorded a double bogey 6. (As cruel fate would have it, Cooper eventually missed the cut—by two shots.)

When the golfer finished the hole, his caddie took the ball and was about to toss it to a spectator when Cooper stopped him and said, "Don't give that ball away. That's the longest ball in the history of golf."

Most Feet Climbed Up a Tree to Retrieve an Errant Shot in a U.S. Open

25 feet
Nick Faldo, 1992
Pebble Beach Golf Links

The par-5, 464-yard 14th hole at Pebble Beach Golf Links is a particularly nasty hole—a narrow dogleg right with a couple of huge oaks guarding the entrance to an elevated green. It was in one of these old seaside trees that Nick Faldo reached the height of embarrassment in his otherwise outstanding career.

On the final day of the 1992 U.S. Open, Faldo mis-hit his 9-iron approach to the green. His ball headed straight into a big oak, but no one saw it come down. So the distinguished British golfer decided to do something most un-British—climb up the tree in hopes of finding his ball.

Faldo started his journey on the lower branches, shaking the limbs at every stop and going successively higher and higher. At one point, the Tarzan-like golfer stopped to yell down to the gallery, "Where the hell is Jane?"

He eventually got up to 25 feet, but he failed to find his ball. Apparently, it was still stuck in the thicker branches above. Faldo eventually had to play a provisional ball and scored a triple bogey 8 on the hole.

After the round, a chagrined Faldo said, "I haven't climbed a tree like that since I was a kid in knee pants."

Highest Score on a Par-3 Hole by a Hall of Famer

11
Ben Hogan
1946 Jacksonville Open

It hardly seems possible that one of the top players of all time could have stumbled so badly at such a short par 3.

But in the third round of the Jacksonville Open at Hyde Park Golf Course, Ben Hogan shot an atrocious 11 on the 150-yard seventh hole.

He had started the day one shot out of the lead and proceeded to par the first six holes. On the seventh hole—which featured a green that was flat on the right side and sloped on the left—Hogan lofted his tee shot purposely toward the left because he wanted to leave himself an uphill putt. He thought he had hit a fine shot.

But the ball hit the green and bounced off, prompting his caddie to say, "Mr. Hogan, I think we are in the lake."

A disbelieving Hogan shot back, "What lake?"

Although he had played the course four times, he wasn't aware of any water on the left side. But then he discovered that trees were shielding the lake from the tee. After searching for his ball, he found it in two inches of water.

Thinking it wouldn't be too difficult to hit it out of the water, Hogan rolled up a pants leg and swatted the ball. It flew out of the water, but struck the bank and trickled back into the drink again.

Again Hogan swung. And again the results were the same. By this time the water had muddied so badly that he couldn't find his ball. So Hogan trudged back to the drop area to play another ball—and launched that one into the lake too.

Eventually he hit a ball onto the green and two-putted for his inglorious 11. He finished the round with an 82 that put him out of the running.

When Hogan returned to his hotel room, his wife Valerie asked him how he had played.

"I told her I had taken an 11 on a par-3 hole," Hogan recalled, "but she didn't believe me.

"We were in a corner room and the windows were open and about that time the voice of a newsboy came floating up. He was shouting, 'Extra! Extra! Ben Hogan takes an 11 on a par-3 hole!'

"Only then did Valerie believe me."

Most Times Being Beaten by an Opponent's Hole-Out

4 times
Greg Norman
1986–90

If ever there's a "Heartbreak Kid" in golf, it's Greg Norman. He's lost four tournaments on the last hole when his opponents holed out incredible shots from off the green. Two of those shots prevented Norman from winning majors.

Norman's first heartbreak happened at the 1986

PGA Championship at Inverness. Norman, who had led almost the entire day, was on the 18th green waiting to putt for an apparent victory. But then, in one of the classic shots in tournament history, Bob Tway blasted his ball into the cup from a greenside bunker to claim the title. No golfer had ever chipped in on the 72nd hole to win a major championship before.

At the very next major, the 1987 Masters, it happened again when Larry Mize holed out during a playoff with Norman. The Shark had put his ball on the 11th green while Mize had missed far to the right. Mize faced a 140-foot chip to a very slick green at a pin cut close to a pond.

"I didn't think Larry would get down in two from there," Norman recalled. "And I was right. Unfortunately, he got down in one."

Norman's heartbreak should have been enough for any mortal to endure, but there was more suffering to follow. At the 1990 Nestle Invitational, Norman was holding a one-shot lead as he stood on Bay Hill's 18th tee. Up ahead of him, in the fairway, Robert Gamez stood with a 7-iron, facing a 176-yard shot over water.

Norman then watched in disbelief as Gamez holed out the fairway shot for a stunning eagle. When Norman couldn't make a birdie, yet another championship was lost on an opponent's dramatic hole-out.

One month later, Norman was victimized by yet another spectacular shot. This time he had just finished making birdie on the difficult 18th hole at the USF&G Classic, pulling into a tie with David Frost. Frost, who had to make par on the final hole to get into a playoff with Norman, looked like he didn't stand a chance when he hit his second shot into a difficult bunker. But Frost belted his ball out of the bunker perfectly and into the cup for an amazing tourney-winning birdie. All Norman could do was shake his head in stunned disbelief.

Of the four, Mize's chip-in was the most difficult pill to swallow "because it came right on the heels of Bob Tway's," Norman recalled. "I would say Larry Mize's position was a hundredfold worse than Tway's. I thought I was totally in control of the situation. Mize was definitely the hardest to take."

Most Strokes Taken by a Foursome in an 18-Hole Round

836 strokes
Angelo Spagnolo (257), Jack Pulford (208), Joel Mosser (192), and Kelly Ireland (179), 1984 TPC at Sawgrass

Can a weekend golfer shoot 179 and be the low player in his foursome—by 13 strokes?

Only if he is the best of the four worst avid golfers in America, as determined by *Golf Digest* magazine, and he is playing one of the toughest courses in the world, the TPC at Sawgrass.

Kelly Ireland had the lowest score of an awfully awesome foursome that, on scout's honor, tried to play their best and shot a woeful combined score of 836. That figures out to an average of 209 for 18 holes, or nearly 12 strokes a hole.

Ireland, 41, a trial lawyer from Tyler, Texas; Joel Mosser, 45, a stockbroker from Aurora, Colorado; Jack Pulford, 48, a restaurant owner from Moline, Illinois; and Angelo Spagnolo, 31, a grocery store manager from Fayette City, Pennsylvania, met at the invitation of *Golf Digest* to decide who was America's worst golfer.

Clearly, it was Spagnolo.

But it wasn't easy to achieve such a shameful title. The foursome accounted for 17 whiffs, 102 balls in the water, 124 penalty strokes, no greens in regulation, and no pars. The best score was a bogey, which happened once, and the next best was a double bogey, which happened eight times.

The golfers' scores were fairly close going into the 17th hole, the famed par-3, 138-yard island green at Sawgrass. There, Spagnolo left the others far ahead.

He took an incredibly pitiful 66 on the hole! He plunked 27 balls into the water, including seven shots that actually hit the green but bounded over into the drink on the other side. Eventually, he had to wave the white flag and putt all the way along the cart path, over the narrow bridge, and onto the green, where he finally got down after three putting. It took the hacker 40 minutes to play the hole.

"After that, the wheels came off a bit," Spagnolo said, explaining why he made 22 on the 18th and final hole.

Meanwhile, Ireland wasn't crowing about being the "medalist" of the four. "I've never seen anything as tough in my life," he said of the course. "On the 11th [a 529-yard par 5], I used every club in my bag—every single one. I was hitting 24 before I got to the fairway."

Most Consecutive Holes Chipped in Cross-Handed

3 consecutive holes
Guy Yaste, 1969
Pensacola Country Club
Pensacola, Florida

Fellow golfers always poked fun at Guy Yaste for his weird cross-handed grip. But Yaste got the last laugh on his playing partners during an extraordinary round at the Pensacola Country Club.

After parring the first hole, the 78-year-old golfer got into trouble on the par-3, 180-yard second hole. Two bad shots left him short of the green. But he lofted his third shot perfectly and it rolled into the cup to save par. At the par-4, 345-yard third hole, Yaste couldn't believe his good fortune when he chipped in again, this time for a birdie.

Now came the fourth hole, a long par-4 420-yarder. After three shots, Yaste was still lying short of the green. Could I possibly chip in again? he wondered. He got his answer seconds later. Incredibly, Yaste holed out for the third consecutive time! He had saved another par.

He shot 37-42-79 for the day, and missed shooting his age by just one stroke.

Most Consecutive Shots in Which a Ball Was Lodged in a Tree

2 consecutive shots
Fred Walker, 1985
St. Jean DeMantha Golf Club
St. Jean DeMantha, Quebec

The trees at St. Jean DeMantha Golf Club have not been terribly kind to Fred Walker of Rawdon, Quebec.

During a forgettable round, Walker hit a shot that stuck in a branch of one of the offending trees. He started to take an unplayable lie, but since the ball was staring at him right at eye level, Walker decided to take a baseball swing at it.

The ball zoomed out of the branches—and made a beeline for another tree 30 yards away. Once again, the ball got snagged in a branch.

Wishing he had a chain saw, Walker dropped a new ball and took an unplayable lie penalty.

Longest Drive by a Senior

515 yards
Mike Austin
1974 U.S. Seniors Open

When pro Mike Austin was 64 years old, he shocked the golfing world by launching what is still the longest drive in Senior PGA Tour history—a 515-yard monster during the 1974 U.S. Seniors Open at the Wildwood Golf Club in Las Vegas.

Aided by a 35-MPH tail wind, the ball soared over the fairway and landed 65 yards past the green on the par-4, 450-yard fifth hole.

In 1993, Austin, who at the age of 82 was still teaching the game five days a week at the Studio City (California) Golf and Tennis Club, recounted his memorable shot: "What I remember is that after chipping back to the green, I three-putted for a damn bogey. But it was one hell of a drive, wasn't it?"

2

Astounding Feats

Most Golf Balls Hit to the Green While Dancing

12 golf balls
Fred Astaire, 1938
Pasadena, California

Although recognized as one of the world's greatest dancers, Fred Astaire was also a fine golfer—and he proved his prowess with both his club and his feet in a remarkable dance scene in the 1938 film *Carefree*.

The script called for Astaire, at a golf club, to dance atop tables and furniture, glide down halls, bound out onto the terrace, and tap his way to the practice range where he was to hit a dozen golf balls while still dancing.

To make the golfing portion of the dance routine—which was shot on a course in Pasadena—more compelling, Astaire and director Mark Sandrich decided to shoot it as one continuous scene. There would be no stopping, no cuts.

The camera started rolling. With music blaring from an outdoor loudspeaker to help him keep a beat, Astaire grabbed a driver and tap-danced his way up to a line of 12 teed-up balls. Moving to the music, Astaire deftly and rhythmically kept dancing while whacking the balls in succession toward a practice green. He didn't miss a beat—or a ball. It was a perfect take.

When some members of the crew went to retrieve the balls, they were astounded at what they saw. All dozen balls were lying on the green—within eight feet of each other!

Coldest Round Ever Played

−27° F
Larry Lujack, 1985
Buffalo Grove Golf Club
Buffalo Grove, Illinois

In weather fit for neither man nor beast, Chicago radio personality Larry Lujack donned arctic gear and played a bone-chilling, teeth-rattling round of golf with the temperature of −27°F—and a wind chill of a deadly −75°F!

It was bitterly cold in the Windy City when Lujack awakened one Sunday morning in January 1985 and figured he couldn't go another day without a round of golf. He tumbled out of bed and was at nearby Buffalo Grove Golf Club at 7:30 A.M. Obviously he didn't need to call in advance to reserve a tee time.

Bundled in layer after layer of winter survival gear, Lujack trudged for the next five hours in record low temperatures and biting arctic wind while swatting a golf ball around the barren course. With the bulky clothes, it was a little cumbersome to swing the club, but the ball carried well because it bounced on the frozen tundra.

Lujack said he played pretty well, losing just three balls under nearly intolerable conditions. But he wasn't sure what he shot. "The wind blew the scorecard out of my hand on the 13th hole and there was no way I could catch it," he said. "I think I shot between 90 and 95."

When last seen, the scorecard was spiraling toward the east. "It probably blew to Cleveland," he added.

Lujack said he was proudest that he survived without the aid of a single Saint Bernard rescue. "Plowing through deep snow for five hours is tough," he admitted. "When I staggered into the clubhouse, my legs felt like I'd just jogged 200 miles through molasses. I had to lie down."

Most Golfers to Shoot Their Exact Weight in the Same Round

2 golfers
Bob Struble and Mark Felger, 1977
Cazenovia Golf Course
Buffalo, New York

Two Buffalo teenagers—Bob Struble, 14, and his friend Mark Felger, 13—shot 90 and 103, respectively, at the Cazenovia Golf Course. The boys looked at their scorecard and then at each other. Those numbers seemed mighty familiar.

So they hurried to the locker room and jumped on the scale. Sure enough, each teen had shot his exact weight!

Most Countries Played in One Day by a Golfer

5 countries
Simon Clough and Boris Janjic, 1992

Golfers Simon Clough and Boris Janjic played a round of golf in five different countries—in one day!

On June 12, 1992, they played rounds in France, Luxembourg, Germany, Holland, and Belgium.

Clough was an English golf pro at Bossenstein Golf Club in Belgium. Janjic was an Australian pro at Henry-Chapelle Golf & Business Club, also in Belgium. While relaxing at the 19th hole, the two decided to see how many countries they could play in one day. So, with the help of selected golf courses that agreed to give them preferential treatment on the links, Clough and Janjic set out to establish a world record. Attesting to the legitimacy of their odyssey was a member of the Belgian Golfers Union, who acted as an official referee.

At each course, the players golfed as fast as they could—averaging a little more than two hours a round—with their wives riding in carts that carried the clubs. As soon as they finished their round, the pros hopped into their car and zoomed off to the next course in another country.

Amazingly, Clough and Janjic managed to accomplish their feat in 16 hours and 35 minutes—including the time it took to drive the total distance of 273 miles between courses.

For their 90 holes, they had an aggregate score of 772—an average of 77.2 per round each. But if Clough was tired from all that golf and travel, he didn't show it. He set a course record at the final stop.

Lowest Round Shot in Desert Boots

69
Craig Stadler, 1975
Los Angeles Country Club
Los Angeles, California

When Craig Stadler was a member of the University of Southern California golf team, he shared a rental house near the campus with teammate Scott Simpson—who also later turned pro—and three other students.

The guys didn't realize they had forgotten to pay

their utility bill until one day they received a notice from the power company that the electricity would be shut off unless payment was received by noon the next day. The deadline was also the day for USC's golf match with archrival UCLA.

After picking straws, Stadler was the unlucky household member chosen to pay the bill. The next day—clad in an old shirt, slacks, and desert boots— he went to the power company office in downtown L.A. and stood in line for nearly an hour before taking care of the bill. Then he frantically drove across town to the Los Angeles Country Club.

Stadler parked his car, jumped a hedge, and arrived at the first tee with just a minute to spare. In his hurry he left his golf shoes in the car and didn't have time to go back and get them. Still wearing his desert boots, he took three quick practice swings and then started the round.

Apparently, the golf shoes weren't that big a deal—Stadler led his team to victory, shooting a three-under-par 69.

Biggest Alligator Flipped Over by a Golfer

6-foot alligator
Andy Bean, 1975
PGA Tour Qualifying School
Disney World Golf Resort

Georgia-born Andy Bean isn't the least bit fazed by alligators sunning themselves along the banks of southern golf course ponds. In fact, once he even grabbed a gator by the tail during a golf match.

It happened in 1975, when Bean was playing in the PGA Tour Qualifying School at Disney World. He and his playing partner, Sandy Galbraith, spotted a gator climbing out of a pond.

"Hey," said a startled Galbraith, "look at that!"

"Aw, that ain't nothin' but an ol' gator," said Bean. "He's harmless."

"It doesn't look harmless to me," a nervous Galbraith retorted, cautiously eyeing the menacing six-foot reptile.

"Watch," said Bean. "I'll show you it's harmless."

With that, Bean dropped his bag and crept up behind the gator. Suddenly, the 6'4", 225-pound golfer grabbed the beast by its tail and flipped it over easily.

The startled alligator angrily turned back onto its feet and thrashed its powerful tail until Bean released it. The gator then scurried into the pond, still unsure what had happened. It had just been Beaned.

Longest Weekly Round-Trip Commute to Play Golf

550 miles
Tom Harold, 1990–present
Australia

Tom Harold loves golf so much he's willing to go through hell and high water to get to the course.

Most weekends, Harold powers a boat across six miles of shark-infested ocean, motorbikes through more than 250 bumpy miles of Australia's treacherous wilderness, and then drives another 20 miles by car— just to hit the links at the nearest golf course.

It's a harried 550-mile round-trip journey that takes anywhere from 8 to 11 hours each way to complete.

"I'll do anything for a game of golf," said the 35-year-old elementary school teacher, who lives on Goulburn Island, a remote aboriginal community six miles off Australia's northern coast. "It's a pleasant, peaceful, idyllic, tropical setting," he added. "The only thing missing is a golf course."

So on Friday afternoons after school he heads for the closest course—275 miles away in the city of Darwin. With a motorbike in his dinghy, Harold arrives at the mainland after a two-hour boat trip. He pulls out his motorbike, hides his boat under some brush, and then embarks on a grueling seven-hour, 250-mile ride over potholed dirt roads often used by wild boar and buffalo. Harold arrives at a friend's home around midnight, collapsing into bed to rest his jarred spine and weary muscles. On Saturday morning, his friend drives him the final 20 miles to the course.

Harold plays 18 holes on Saturday and nine on Sunday before retracing the arduous trek back home. "The worst part of the round-trip is the final bit—when I have to do the sea crossing to the island in the dark," he said.

"Then, as the waves crash against my boat, I sometimes swear to myself never to make this crazy journey again. But within a few days, as the bruises get less painful, I'm soon craving another game of golf."

Most Brothers to Turn Pro

6 brothers
Mike, Frank, Joe, Phil, Doug, and Jim Turnesa,
1930s and '40s

Never before has any one family produced such a large number of outstanding golfers. The Turnesas— Mike, Frank, Joe, Phil, Doug, and Jim—all played on the PGA Tour during the 1930s and 1940s. However, none of them ever won a major title.

A seventh brother, Willie, bucked the trend and refused to become a pro golfer. Instead, he remained a world-class amateur, winning the U.S. Amateur championship in 1938 and the British Amateur in 1947.

Fastest 18-Hole Round with a Single Ball

11 minutes, 24 seconds
Members of Stonecreek, The Golf Club, 1992
Paradise Valley, Arizona

Ninety-one members of Stonecreek, The Golf Club set a world record for the fastest round of "relay golf" with a single ball—11 minutes, 24 seconds.

The golfers stationed themselves at various intervals from the first tee to the 18th green and, in relay fashion, propelled the ball around their 6,506-yard course.

If a ball was hit into a hazard, it was abandoned and the round was started over. In 44 attempts, the ball never made it around the course. After being holed out, the ball was thrown from the green to the next tee to speed up the effort.

The ball that completed the round the fastest was the one used on the 50th attempt. The real slowpoke ball—the worst of the 16 that finished—still made the trip around the course in just over 17 minutes.

Most Holes Played in One Day Equal to a Golfer's Age

81
Dr. R. C. Spangler, 1965
Morgantown, West Virginia

It was a tradition that Dr. R. C. Spangler started when he turned 66 years old. To celebrate his birthday on August 1, he played 66 holes to match his age.

On each birthday thereafter, he increased the number of holes he played by one. By the time he reached his 81st birthday in 1965, Dr. Spangler still had enough spunk left to play 81 holes.

The ex-professor of botany and biology at West Virginia University used only a driver and an adjustable iron to play his rounds.

Most Major Tournament Winners Out of One Qualifying School

4 tournament winners
Tom Watson, Lanny Wadkins,
David Graham, and John Mahaffey
Class of 1971

Perhaps never in the history of golf was there as talented a group of Q-school grads as the ones who earned their PGA Tour cards in 1971. Combined, Tom Watson, Lanny Wadkins, David Graham, and John Mahaffey have gone on to win a total of 12 majors. Bolstered by Watson's 32 victories, the four golfers have won 80 tournaments—more than the victories of the graduates of the next 10 classes combined.

Among the accomplishments of the four 1971 grads are: two U.S. Open wins—Graham and Watson (1981 and 1982, respectively); two Masters titles—Watson (1977 and 1981); three PGA championships—Wadkins, Mahaffey, and Graham (1977, 1978, and 1979, respectively); and five British Opens—Watson (1975, 1977, 1980, 1982, and 1983).

What's surprising about the class of '71 is that none of the Big Four finished as a medalist at the school. That honor went to Bob Zender of Skokie, Illinois, who beat runner-up Wadkins by three shots. Zender never won a tournament and now is in the security business in Chicago.

A notable member of the Class of '71 was former major league outfielder Ken Harrelson, who had just finished his nine-year baseball career with the Cleveland Indians. He tried to qualify as a Tour pro because, he said, "nothing could be worse than playing for the Cleveland Indians."

Unfortunately, Harrelson flunked Q-school.

Most Eagles by One Golfer on One Hole

2 eagles
Fred Class, 1974
Lake Venice Golf Club
Venice, Florida

Amateur Fred Class scored two eagles on the same hole—by playing two balls.

Class, of Kitchener, Ontario, accomplished this amazing feat at the Lake Venice Golf Club. Because he was a single on the course, he decided to give his game a little extra work by playing two balls.

At the par-4, 357-yard 11th hole, he hit two outstanding tee shots, both landing within five feet of each other in the center of the fairway. He swatted the first ball with a 9-iron and watched as the ball went into the hole on the fly. He then hit his second ball with the same 9-iron. Remarkably, it was a carbon copy of the first shot. The ball rose into the air and landed right in the hole!

Most Lessons Given by a Teaching Pro in an Average Year

3,000 (estimated)
Ernest Jones, 1924–38
New York

Ernest Jones was the most prolific golf instructor in American history. In his prime, in the 1920s and 1930s, he was averaging 3,000 lessons a year.

Jones was an exceptional English pro who lost his right leg below the knee while in the British army during World War I. He emigrated to the United States in 1924 and became almost as popular as the country's most famous golf instructor at the time, Tommy Armour.

Armour—winner of the U.S. Open, British Open, and PGA Championship—gave about 300 lessons a year. For a fee of up to $100 a lesson, Armour would instruct his wealthy students as he sat under a beach umbrella at the practice range.

Jones's style was totally unorthodox. He did his teaching indoors for no more than $5 a lesson—primarily in a studio that had been a storage room on the seventh floor of a building in midtown Manhattan. He was a classic workaholic, scheduling lessons from 9:30 A.M. to 6 P.M., refusing to stop for lunch. He taught everyone from top executives to secretaries, from lawyers to cab drivers.

Even after he left his classroom, he sometimes wouldn't quit teaching. He was known to give an impromptu free lesson in the rotunda of the Grand Central Terminal while waiting for the train to take him home to Glen Head, Long Island.

If his teaching style was totally unlike almost every other instructor's in America, so was his concept of the golf swing. He didn't dissect the golf swing into parts such as the backswing or the positions of the left arm, knees, and feet. He taught one concept—the swing of the clubhead. He didn't care about form or style. Jones dismissed teaching all the other points of the swing by saying, "If you dissect a cat, you'll have blood and guts and bones all over the place. But you won't have a cat."

3

Odd Tournament Records

Most Golfers Named Bobby Jones in One Tournament

78 Bobby Joneses
Bobby Jones Open, 1992
Cordova Club
Cordova, Tennessee

There's never any doubt who will win the Annual Bobby Jones Open. And there's never any doubt who will finish last. That's because every golfer in the field is named Bobby Jones.

In fact, the only requirement to play in the event is that your name must be Bob, Bobby, Robert, Roberta, or Bobbie Jones. The tournament pays homage to Robert Tyre Jones, the famed golfer who won four U.S. Opens.

"Being a Bob Jones, I wondered how many of us there were," said founder Bob Jones, owner of a computer business in Detroit. "I found four others in the phone book and we had our first tournament in 1979." Ever since word of the tournament spread, Bob Joneses from all over the country and as far away as England and Australia have been teeing up with the Joneses.

The annual event raises money for the Beaumont Hospital, which is dedicated to finding a cure for syringomyelia, a fatal disease that attacks the nervous system. The disease killed the Hall of Fame golfer.

To keep track of all the Bobby Joneses in the tourney, each player has a nickname such as Sandtrap, Computer Bob, Chrysler, and 1992's winner, Iron Man, who beat 77 other Bob Joneses. Famed golf course architects Robert Trent Jones and Robert Trent Jones, Jr., have played. And so have three generations of a family of Bob Joneses from Memphis, nicknamed Banker 1, his son Viking 1, and grandson Viking 2.

Incidentally, the 1992 event was played at the Cordova Club, which was developed by, you guessed it, Bob Jones.

Most Shots Over Par on a Hole After Going to the Toilet in a Major Tournament

3 shots over par
Jack Nicklaus
1978 U.S. Open

Jack Nicklaus was near the lead in the third round of the 1978 U.S. Open when he reached the 13th hole at Cherry Hills Country Club. After hitting his tee shot, he hurried into a nearby portable toilet to answer a very urgent call from nature.

When he came back out, Nicklaus promptly flubbed his shot from the middle of the fairway. He messed up his recovery shot and wound up taking an uncharacteristic seven on the par-4 hole. Thanks to his triple bogey, the Golden Bear quickly faded from contention.

After the round, Nicklaus was beckoned to the media room and asked for an explanation. The superstar coughed a couple of times, looked shamefacedly around the room, then spoke. "I don't know how this is going to look in print, but I never did get my mind back on what I was doing after I went to the toilet."

So, was he sorry that he made the pit stop?

"No," he replied. "I had to go."

Most Topless Dancers Attending a Golf Tournament

30 topless dancers
Forest Creek Golf Course, 1990–1992
Round Rock, Texas

Topless dancers were par for the course during several tournaments sponsored by Austin nightclubs.

In the events, held at nearby Forest Creek between 1990 and 1992, as many as 30 of the clubs' entertainers turned out to spice up the play of the male golfers. Wearing nothing but thong bikini bottoms, the bare-breasted women drove golf carts around the course, served food and drinks, and wrecked the concentration of almost every golfer—none of whom complained.

"It seemed that the more distracted we were, the more tips we gave them," said one golfer.

Beamed a fellow competitor, "We had the breast of both worlds—golf and women."

But residents of Round Rock, which owns the course, teed off against city officials for allowing topless women on the links.

Resident Arvella Goodrum said she was driving by the course when she noticed two women at the eighth tee, obviously missing some parts of their clothing. In fact, from the road, it looked to Arvella like they were missing all their clothes.

"I was shocked," she said. "I turned around and went back to see if I really saw what I thought I saw. The girls were topless, but they did have skimpy little bottoms on."

Mrs. Goodrum and other residents lodged so many complaints that the city council wrote up an ordinance that would prohibit toplessness on the golf course.

Meanwhile, Howard Lennett, manager of Sugar's Uptown Cabaret—one of three topless clubs that sponsored the tournaments—agreed to reevaluate the women's participation in the events. "After all," he explained, "we are concerned about our public image."

Most Holes Played by a Golfer Who Failed to Realize She Was Competing in the Olympics

9 holes
Margaret Abbot
1900 Paris Games

American Margaret Abbot was the first and only winner in women's Olympic golf. She was also the first and only winner who didn't know she was playing in the Olympics!

In 1900, when Margaret was a 21-year-old art student abroad in Paris, the Olympic Committee invited athletes to the Games held in the City of Lights. Among the Olympic medal sports was women's golf.

While growing up in the United States, Margaret had learned the game at Shinnecock Hills and many other courses by playing with her mother, Mary Abbot. The 5'11" Margaret was a decent golfer with a long, sweeping swing and a precise putting touch.

She and her mother were among the 10 women golfers who showed up for the one-round women's Olympic tournament at the Pau Golf Club. Margaret could hardly contain her laughter when she saw her French competitors. They were all dressed with a sophisticated elegance more suited for a night on the town than a day on the links. The Frenchwomen arrived at the club wearing high heels and tight skirts. Incredibly, that's the garb they played in!

Margaret, clad in more traditional, comfortable golf wear, completely outclassed the rest of the field. Not that she was any great shakes with a club. But she was better than all the rest, shooting an 11-over-par 47 to win the nine-hole tourney. Another American, Pauline Whittier, was second, carding a 49.

Years later, Margaret confessed to friends and relatives that she didn't realize she was participating in the Olympics. She played the entire round thinking she was competing in the French Amateur championship. Not until the awards ceremony did it dawn on her that she had competed in the Olympics.

It's hardly surprising that, after such a bizarre beginning, golf was discontinued as an Olympic sport.

Most Holes Played Barefoot at the Masters

18 holes
Sam Snead, 1942
Augusta National

Sam Snead was born and raised in the Virginia mountains at a time and place where shoes were treated in much the same manner as suits—to be worn only on Sundays for church. Snead learned to play golf barefoot, eschewing such fancy trappings as spikes. He even advocated playing shoeless as a great aid in learning proper balance.

At the 1942 Masters, playing a practice round at the revered Augusta National, Snead went the entire 18 holes barefoot. "Shucks," he once said, "I'm really 15 years younger than my birth certificate shows. In Virginia, we don't count the years you go barefoot."

Most Consecutive Tournaments Played Without Winning a Cent

88 consecutive tournaments
Becky Larson, 1985–90

Perhaps a person with less tenacity would have figured that golf was the wrong career. But Becky Larson was going to win a paycheck from an LPGA tournament if it took her a lifetime. Some thought it might.

Larson played five years and 88 tournaments without earning a nickel in winnings. Her moneyless streak finally ended in September 1990, when she made the cut and won $283 at the Rail Charity Classic.

On the most lucrative day of her professional career, after five years of futility, she almost lost her chance to collect!

After finally surviving the cut that virtually assured her of her first payday, Larson had a 10:20 A.M. tee time on Sunday, the final day of the tournament. At the appointed time, however, she was nowhere to be found, so her playing partners teed off without her.

As they were preparing to hit their second shots to the first green, a car came screeching into the parking lot. It was Larson. Still in tennis shoes, she hurdled a fence, sprinted to the tee, and, while still catching her breath, hit her opening drive to prevent being disqualified. Had her partners hit their second shots, she would have been dropped from the tournament and not been able to collect a penny.

As it was, the 29-year-old golfer from Watertown, South Dakota, incurred a two-shot penalty for being late but was allowed to finish the round. Her excuse for nearly blowing her first paycheck? She said she had simply miscalculated her tee time. After all, she hadn't had to play on a Sunday in a tournament in five years.

"It was definitely a bozo move," said Larson, who shot an 80 and finished third from last place. "I would have hated to call my dad and tell him that after finally making a check, I blew it."

Longest Time Between Tournament Victories

12 years, 7 months
Howard Twitty, 1980-93

In 1980, after winning the Sammy Davis, Jr. Greater Hartford Open and finishing the year 14th on the money list, Howard Twitty thought he was at the peak of his career.

Instead, he wallowed in the valley of a victory drought that didn't end until nearly 13 years later, when the 44-year-old veteran captured the 1993 Hawaiian Open by four strokes. He won $216,000—which was more than his combined earnings in any one season with the exception of 1992.

The first person to greet the victor when he came off the green was his daughter, Jocelyn, who was born the same year Twitty had last won. She had never seen her father win a tournament.

"This is very, very special," Twitty said. "There are a lot of emotions, an awful, awful lot of emotions. With my daughter being here to see it, it's one of the special days of my life."

Oldest Minimum Age for Entering
a Tournament

80 years old
Bill Gabriel Over-80 Tourney, 1991–present
Rossmoor Retirement Community
Walnut Creek, California

Arnold Palmer can't play in this one yet. Neither can Miller Barber. But George Burns is welcome.

You have to be an octogenarian or older to play in the Bill Gabriel Over-80 Tourney.

The annual event was started in 1991 by Bill Gabriel when he was 90 years old. The energetic resident of the Rossmoor retirement community of 10,000 senior citizens has been an avid golfer since he first picked up a set of clubs at the age of 60.

"The tournament came about after one of our residents died while on the driving range and some friends were trying to figure out a way to honor his memory," said Rossmoor golf pro Norm Oliver. "But then Bill said the best thing they could do would be a memorial for the living. So he put up $500 in prize money and started his Over-80 Tourney."

The event, held each October, features about 50 players, both men and women. So far, the oldest participant has been 94 years young. The tourney, which runs for two weeks, is eclectic. That means the contestants can play more than once and can turn in their best scores for each hole, 1 through 18.

"They're not bad players," said Oliver. "One of the golfers shot a hole in one." The best scores, with handicap, have been 29 for nine holes and 62 for a full round.

Gabriel foresees his tournament eventually becoming national with 80-and-overs from all around the country participating. "Maybe a sponsor will appear," he said. "It would be a natural for Geritol."

Highest Score Shot in a 36-Hole British Open Qualifier

221
Walter Danecki
1965 British Open

Walter Danecki was a weekend hacker who lacked golfing skills but not gumption. This 47-year-old postal clerk from Milwaukee managed to play in the British Open qualifier!

Danecki had planned a July vacation in England. By chance, he heard he was going to be in the country the same time as the British Open. Suddenly, a light bulb clicked on in his head. Why not do something that would really impress his pals back in Milwaukee? Why not enter the British Open, just to shock his friends who would see his name in the scoring summary for the qualifying event?

And so he sent in his application. Amazingly, the tournament officials accepted it. They reasoned that, although they had never heard of Walter Danecki, he must be a new member of the PGA Tour. With no questions asked, the officials gave him his tee time for the 36-hole qualifier.

Danecki, who seldom broke 100 back in Milwaukee, then went out and shot a dreadful 108-113—that's 71 over par—at the qualifier at Hillside Golf Course in Southport, England.

Tournament officials were not amused when they discovered a duffer in their midst. Talking with reporters after his round, Danecki said, "I can't get into a lot of tournaments in my part of the country, so I thought I would come over here and win a big one. Then they would have to let me in the others."

Best Score of a One-Hole Match Between a Bride and Groom

Bogey 6 (tie)
Christyne Curley Velez and Bill Velez, 1992
Sterling Farms Golf Club
Stamford, Connecticut

To kick off their wedding reception, bride Christyne Curley Velez, a 31-handicapper, challenged her new husband, Bill Velez, a 26-handicapper, to a one-hole match on the par-5, 515-yard 18th hole at Sterling Farms Golf Club.

The wedding guests cheered the newlyweds as they headed for the tee. Still wearing her floor-length chiffon wedding gown and wielding her Big Bertha, Christyne banged her tee shot 175 yards down the right side of the fairway. Velez, wearing tux and tails, outgunned her by 25 yards with a 200-yard drive.

Christyne eventually reached the back fringe of the green in four shots, then nearly got her par when her chip shot struck the flag and bounced a few inches from the hole. She made a bogey 6—and put the pressure squarely on the groom, who was languishing in a greenside bunker in three shots.

Bill, though, managed to extricate himself with a blast that put the ball onto the green in 4, 30 feet from the hole. Now came the big question: Would he nail the long putt and upstage his wife only minutes after exchanging their wedding vows? Or would he do the gentlemanly thing and three-putt, making the new missus happy in his first official act as a husband?

Bill did neither. Instead, he knocked his first putt 29 feet and then made the one-foot tap-in for a bogey.

The newlyweds had tied not only the knot but also the match.

Most Consecutive Rounds a Major Tournament Winner Shot the Same Score

4 consecutive rounds
Denny Shute
1933 British Open

Playing in the Open at St. Andrews, Scotland, Denny Shute won in a playoff over American Craig Wood. Shute's regulation four rounds, though, may have been even more noteworthy than his championship. Shute recorded the same tally all four days, 73-73-73-73, for a 292 total.

Most Miles a Pro Rode on the Back of a Harley to Make a Tournament Tee-Off Time

3 miles
Gary Player, 1980
Akron, Ohio

Gary Player almost didn't make it on time to the third round of the 1980 World Series of Golf.

Driving a courtesy car himself, Player left his downtown Akron hotel at what he thought was plenty early to make his tee time at the Firestone Country

Club. But the traffic was a terrible mess. Three miles from the course, cars were at a standstill. Player nervously looked at his watch and saw he had only 25 minutes until his name would be called on the first tee.

The diminutive South African, a physical fitness fanatic, calculated it would take him 18 minutes to run the three miles, which would give him seven minutes to catch his breath before he had to tee off. So he abandoned his car at the side of the road and started to run.

Player had gone only a few yards when he spied a group of black-jacketed motorcyclists. He hurriedly approached them and offered to fill the gas tanks of all the cycles if one of them would take him to the course.

"Jump on, man," said the leader, an overweight, bearded biker, as he revved up his high-handlebarred Harley-Davidson. The desperate golfer, who had never been on a motorcycle before, hopped on. Clutching the biker's jacket, Player roared off on the ride of his life.

Twice they were stopped by Akron police as they weaved through traffic and drove on the wrong side of the road. Twice Player talked his way out of a ticket. With a few minutes to spare, the bike reached the gate at Firestone.

"A guard put his hand up to stop us," Player recalled, "but I waved at him and told the driver to keep going." The biker finally screeched to a stop in front of the locker room, much to Player's relief. The two settled on a fee of $20 for the frenzied ride.

"Imagine," said Player who shot a 3-under-par 69 for the round. "Only $20. Why, he had long greasy hair and a big beard, and I could have kissed him."

Most Strokes Improved After Overcoming a Case of the Nerves in One's First Major Tournament

9 strokes
Hal Sutton
1981 U.S. Open

As the reigning U.S. Amateur champion, Hal Sutton was invited to play in his first U.S. Open in 1981 at Merion Golf Club in Ardmore, Pennsylvania.

Nervous beyond belief just to be there, the 23-year-old rookie turned into a human blob of Silly Putty because he was playing with his all-time favorite golfer, Jack Nicklaus. "Jack's been my idol ever since I was a junior golfer," Sutton recalled. "I was paired with a guy I idolized all my life and I was petrified, to tell you the truth. He was the next thing to God."

Shaking and sweating, Sutton started the day with a triple bogey, and things didn't improve much over the next several holes. In fact, after seven holes, Sutton was a pitiful eight over par.

Writhing in embarrassment, the young golfer finally summoned up the courage to speak to Nicklaus. "Did anyone ever tell you how intimidating you can be?" Sutton asked.

Nicklaus smiled and replied, "I'm just as nervous as you are, Hal. The only difference is I've got 20 years of experience in controlling it."

Sutton smiled back, and suddenly the enormous pressure he felt began to ease. He began to play like he had in the U.S. Amateur, hitting one crisp shot after another. In a dramatic turnaround, he mastered the last 11 holes of the round, playing them in an impressive one under par. Unfortunately, he still missed the cut with a seven-over-par 78.

"I was an amateur then and I wanted to play like a pro," Sutton recalled. "I never wanted to be put in that position again. I figured I would either get completely out of the game or completely into the game."

Sutton turned pro, and two years later won his first major, the 1983 PGA Championship.

Only U.S. Open Champion Who Declined to Defend His Title

Jerome Dunstan Travers, 1916

Such piddling matters as a U.S. Open trophy never did impress Jerry Dunstan. He was the son of a wealthy family from Upper Montclair, New Jersey, and had a richly deserved reputation as a playboy. He was also a very fine golfer who didn't take the sport all that seriously.

At the 1915 U.S. Open at Baltusrol Golf Club in New Jersey, the 25-year-old Travers entered as an amateur. He played the last six holes of the tournament in one under par—an outstanding score in that era—and beat professional Tom McNamara by a stroke.

Travers took home the trophy. When it came time to defend his title the following year at Minikahda Country Club in Minneapolis, he didn't even bother to go. After all, he had already won the title once.

In fact, Travers never again entered a major golf tournament.

How good could Travers have been? By the time he was 25, he had won four U.S. Amateurs in addition to his U.S. Open title. But to him, the game was never anything more than a diversion.

Highest Score in a Tournament by the Course Architect

80
Ben Crenshaw
1991 Kapalua International

Ben Crenshaw learned a humiliating lesson: you shouldn't design a golf course that you can't master.

Crenshaw teamed with Bill Coore in designing the Kapalua Plantation Course on the Hawaiian island of Maui. The course was finished just in time to host the Kapalua International, an event in which most of the players shot excellent scores the first time they played it.

Crenshaw wasn't one of them. Playing on his own course in tournament competition, he shot a woeful seven-over-par 80.

Youngest Female to Beat Bobby Jones

12 years old
Alexa Sterling, 1908
Atlanta, Georgia

Alexa Sterling was the only female ever to beat the great Bobby Jones. She was just 12 years old! But then, Bobby was only six.

In 1908, the two friends attended a neighborhood party in Atlanta where they were pitted against each other in a six-hole golf competition. The prize for the winner was a small trophy.

Alexa won the match. But Bobby ended up with the trophy. That's because he ran off with it and took it to bed with him that night.

4

Incredible
Holes in One

Most Balls Hit in One Day While Trying to Make an Ace

1,817 balls
Harry Gonder, 1940

Harry Gonder, an American professional, desperately wanted to make a hole in one. So he went out one day in 1940 and tried his hardest. He believed that if he stood at a par-3 tee and hit one ball after another, he was bound to score an ace.

After arriving at a par-3, 160-yard hole, Gonder started flailing away. For 16 grueling hours, he whacked the same shot over and over, hitting more than 100 balls an hour, from sunup to sundown.

But, sadly, not one went into the hole.

His closest shot came on his 1,756th try. The ball headed straight for the flag, took a bounce on the green, rolled directly toward the hole—and died just an agonizing inch from the cup. The devastated Gonder hit another 61 shots, but, discouraged and fatigued, he called it a day after clubbing 1,817 balls.

The National Hole-in-One Foundation calculates a golfer will make an ace every 12,000 tee shots. If those odds had held for Gonder, he would have had to repeat his efforts for another 5½ days before finally scoring his ace.

Highest Score for Shooting an "Ace"

9
Lew Cullum, 1967
Yacht Club Estates Golf Club
St. Petersburg, Florida

Amateur Lew Cullum had to mark down a 9 on his scorecard—for shooting an "ace"!

Cullum, of Largo, Florida, encountered a world of problems on the par-3, 145-yard 11th hole at Yacht Club Estates Golf Club. It started with a flubbed tee shot into the lake surrounding the hole. Then he sent another drive into the drink. And another . . . and another.

On his fifth try, his tee shot cleared the lake, landed neatly on the green—and rolled right into the cup for what would have been an ace had he hit it on his first attempt.

But because of the stroke and distance penalties from his first four errant drives, Cullum ended up shooting a hole in nine.

Most Holes in One on Consecutive Days by a Blind Golfer

2 holes in one
Margaret Waldron, 1990
Long Point Golf Course
Amelia Island, Florida

Although she was legally blind, 74-year-old Margaret Waldron of Jacksonville, Florida, did what many low-handicap golfers with perfect vision have never done—scored a hole in one.

And if that wasn't incredible enough, she aced the same hole the next day—with the same club and the same ball!

Experts have computed the odds against an amateur scoring a hole in one at 12,000 to 1, and no one yet has attempted to establish the likelihood of a blind golfer recording an ace. "To do it twice on the same hole, two days in a row, using the same club and the same ball, makes the odds beyond comprehension," said Long Point golf pro Ed Tucker.

Waldron had lost her vision 10 years earlier to an eye disease. Instead of giving up sports, though, she continued to be an active golfer, relying on her husband, Pete, to line her up and to describe the hole, distance, and playing conditions.

During a round with friends on March 18, 1990, Pete handed Margaret a 7-iron and pointed her toward the flag on Long Point's 87-yard seventh hole. "I hit the ball solidly," Margaret recalled. "One of my friends said, 'Good hit, Margaret. . . . Wow! Its going for the green! It's going toward the hole!'

"Another friend shouted, 'You've got a hole in one!' We all hugged and I felt a great sense of fulfillment. That night, Pete and I celebrated."

When Margaret arrived at the same hole the next day, she took the same 7-iron and once again hit the 87-yard shot perfectly. The ball rolled into the cup for another ace. "When we went back to the clubhouse, I was so proud," Margaret said. "I don't consider myself handicapped. I am challenged to do the best I can with what I have. What else should I do? Sit home and knit? Not me!"

Most Aces in the Same Cup with the Same Ball on the Same Day

2 aces
Jim Whelehan, 1992
Heather Glen Golf Links
Myrtle Beach, South Carolina

On March 1, 1992, Jim Whelehan turned a routine golf outing into one of the rarest days in links history.

On that day, Whelehan, a phone company executive from Rochester, New York, made two holes in one—in the same cup and with the same ball!

Whelehan, 43, a 5-handicapper, was on a golfing vacation at Heather Glen Golf Links, a 27-hole layout in which some holes are used twice. For example, the par-3, 115-yard fourth hole in the first round doubles as the 13th hole in the second round. This was the hole that Whelehan "owned."

Using a 7-iron in the first round, Whelehan lofted his tee shot onto the green and watched it bounce right into the cup for an ace. As if that wasn't thrilling enough, he hit an identical shot with the same club in his second round of the day for another hole in one. "I'm glad I hit good shots both times," he said. "I didn't knock them in off a rake or run them through a sand trap."

Golf Digest, which has logged unusual hole in one stories since 1952, calculated the odds of the feat at one in a million. Added Whelehan, "I believe that good shots end up one foot from the hole and lucky shots go in. I think it was more good fortune than skill."

Most Objects Hit en Route to a Hole in One

4 objects
Ted Barnhouse, 1981
Mountain View Country Club
John Day, Oregon

Amateur Ted Barnhouse hit one of the wackiest aces in golf history. It ricocheted off four objects before plopping into the cup.

It all happened on the par-3, 145-yard fourth hole at Mountain View Country Club in the little Oregon town of John Day where Barnhouse, a cattleman, played most of his golf.

His bizarre ace began with an awful-looking tee shot—a shank that screamed to the right, sailed over a barbed wire fence, and headed into a herd of cows. The ball smacked into the forehead of a startled bovine, then bounced back toward the course.

The shot next hit a sprinkler head, which redirected the ball over the green and into the third object on its zany journey—a parked lawn mower. From there, the ball ricocheted back onto the green and rolled straight for the flagstick. After banging into the pin—the fourth object—the ball dropped into the cup for a crazy hole in one.

Strangest Award for Acing a Hole

Half a car
Art Schmuckal, 1986
Elmbrook Golf Club
Traverse City, Michigan

Art Schmuckal won half a car because he opened his big mouth seconds before scoring a hole in one.

He and his friend Gil McHuron were playing partners in a tournament at Elmbrook Golf Club—an event that offered a new car to anyone who could ace the 170-yard ninth hole.

When they reached number nine, Schmuckal turned to McHuron and suggested that if either aced the hole, they would share the car. His pal agreed. It seemed a harmless remark, especially since Schmuckal had been playing for 25 years without ever scoring an ace.

But there's a first time for everything, and this time the odds finally caught up with Schmuckal. Using his 4-wood off the tee, he knocked the ball into the cup. He jumped up and down, thinking he had won a brand-new car. But then Schmuckal suddenly realized he owned only half a car because of the agreement he had struck with his friend.

"A deal's a deal," said Schmuckal. So, after figuring out the worth of the car, he bought the other half from McHuron. Said Schmuckal, "The front half was already mine, so I bought the back half."

Most Times Scoring a 3 on an "Ace" in One Month

2 times
John Gentile, 1991
Fountaingrove Country Club
Santa Rosa, California

Amateur John Gentile experienced one of the strangest months in golf history in May 1991.

Playing the par-3, 127-yard fifth hole at Fountaingrove Country Club, Gentile mis-hit a tee shot that veered deep into the rough. Assuming it was lost, Gentile teed up a provisional ball, swatted it, and watched in wonder as it hit the green, bounced once, and settled into the cup. But instead of a hole in one, he had to mark down a 3 as the rules required.

Two weeks later, at the same course, Gentile was teeing off on the par-3, 171-yard 12th hole with his 5-iron. But he lifted his head as he swung, topping the ball about 10 feet in front of the tee. So he took a mulligan.

His next tee shot was perfect, bounding into the cup for his second hole in one of the month. Yet, for the second time, he had to score his ace a 3.

Around the clubhouse, Gentile quickly gained an unwanted reputation. Lamented the golfer, "It's hard being known as the guy who can't do it right on the first shot."

Fewest Days After Cataract Surgery to Score an Ace

6 days
Joe Graney, 1992
Heritage Ridge Golf Club
Stuart, Florida

It's amazing what a golfer can do when he can see the ball well. Joe Graney is living testimony.

Just six days after undergoing cataract surgery on his right eye, the 68-year-old golfer scored the first ace in his life. Even more astounding is what happened to Graney six days after the same operation on his left eye. He nailed another hole in one!

"It's getting blasé now," he said with a grin after his second ace. "I can finally see the ball. I was walking around nearly blind for years."

Graney, a 16-handicapper, used a 9-iron to put his ball straight into the cup on the par-3, 110-yard 11th hole for his ace following the first operation. Several weeks later, after his second cataract surgery, he used his 5-iron to send his tee shot on the par-3, 160-yard seventh hole into the cup.

"Most people go all their life without getting a hole in one, and here I've gotten two in about two months," Graney said.

But he doesn't recommend cataract surgery to improve your golf game. "Keep your head down, swing hard, and rip it," he said. "It's luck to have it go into the hole. Sometimes you get on a roll."

Most Generations of a Family to Ace the Same Hole

3 generations
The Fribley family, 1971–91
Pana Country Club
Pana, Illinois

To the Fribley family, scoring a hole in one on the seventh hole at the Pana Country Club has become a tradition. Three generations of the clan have aced it.

In 1971, 65-year-old John Fribley was the first in the family to conquer the par-3, 186-yard hole with a 3-wood. Four years later, his 16-year-old grandson, Scott, who played on the Pana High School golf team, aced the hole. It took 16 years before another member of the family duplicated the feat. In 1991, Judge Joseph Fribley—John's son and Scott's father—used his 4-iron to become the third generation of Fribleys to score a hole in one on lucky number seven.

Longest Roll of a Dead Ball Jolted into the Cup by an Earth Tremor for an Ace

2 inches
Morton Shapiro, 1956
Indian Springs Country Club
Marlton, New Jersey

Morton Shapiro scored an ace thanks to a rare natural phenomenon.

Shapiro, an attorney from Camden, New Jersey, was playing the 130-yard fifth hole at Indian Springs Country Club when he hit his tee shot with considerable backspin.

The ball landed several yards beyond the cup,

but bit into the turf and spun back. As the ball rolled closer and closer toward the hole, Shapiro was all set to jump for joy over his first ace ever. But to his dismay, the ball died just short of the cup by a couple of inches.

Shapiro stood still on the tee, hoping against hope that the ball would, by some miracle, start up again and plunk into the cup. But there seemed no chance of that happening. The ball had definitely stopped. And there was no wind to gently push it into the hole.

As Shapiro headed toward the green, he walked down a swale that momentarily blocked his view of his ball. By the time he could see the hole once again, he was shocked—his ball wasn't there. He hurried to the cup and to his great surprise found the ball inside. By some miracle, the motionless ball got going again and finished the last two inches of its journey into the cup for a hole in one!

Upon further investigation, it appeared that Mother Nature had lent a hand in the ace. About a minute after Shapiro had teed off, the area was hit with a rare earth tremor. The ground shook just enough to start the ball rolling again right into the hole.

Most Number of Sevens Linked to a Hole in One

7
Kent Averett, 1977
Painted Hills Golf Club
Salt Lake City, Utah

The number seven played a big role in the hole in one made by Kent Averett of Cedar City, Utah, at a par-3, 197-yard hole at Painted Hills Golf Club.

It happened on the seventh day of the seventh month of 1977 (7-7-77 if you're keeping the date numerically). Averett made his ace at the seventh hole—at exactly 7:00 P.M. There was a seventh seven linked to his ace. It was the seventh hole-in-one of the year at Painted Hills.

There could have been more sevens if fate had really wanted to have fun. Averett didn't use a 7-iron; he used a 6-iron. And he didn't shoot a 77 that day; he shot a 72. If only he had been drinking a 7-Up before the shot. . . .

Shortest Time Between Dreaming of Scoring an Ace While Playing with a Dead President and Actually Making One

2 months
Vicki Tanigaki, 1989
Sweetwater Country Club
Sugar Land, Texas

Vicki Tanigaki, a 15-handicapper, dreamed that the late John F. Kennedy had invited her to play golf with him and that during their round, she sank a hole in one.

When she awakened the next day, Vicki went straight to the Sweetwater Country Club near Houston and joined the "Hole-in-One-Club." (Members pay $5 to join. It's like an insurance policy. If a member scores an ace, he or she doesn't have to buy drinks for everyone. The club ponies up the money instead.)

Two months later, Vicki played in her first official tournament at the club. And her dream came true—at least part of it. On the par-3, 150-yard seventh hole, Vicki knocked in a hole in one!

Although Kennedy wasn't there, perhaps his spirit was. The name of the tournament was the President's Cup.

Highest Score Deliberately Taken for a Hole in One

3
Ev Hanlon, 1965
Avon Country Club
Avon, Connecticut

Ev Hanlon had his fill of holes in one by the time he made his third ace in 1965 at Avon Country Club. After each of the first two, he had dutifully endured golf's time-honored tradition of the ace-maker buying a round of drinks for all those in the club bar.

It was a tradition that he didn't want to experience again.

So after his 170-yard tee shot on the 11th hole went into the cup for an ace, Hanlon stunned his playing partners by declining their congratulations. He plucked his ball out of the cup and announced to the group that he was declaring an unplayable lie and taking a penalty stroke. Then he proceeded to place the ball a few feet from the cup and tap it in. "Give me a three," he said.

Hanlon, a district engineering manager, explained that he felt there were far better uses for money than splurging it on drinks for the gang. "I'd rather see it go to some kind of charity, or perhaps a caddie scholarship."

Most Holes in One by an Armless Golfer

8 holes in one
Jim Taylor, 1986–present
Golf Green Golf Center
Longview, Washington

Jim Taylor has hit an incredible eight aces—even though he has no arms!

Taylor, an insurance executive, lost both arms in a childhood accident when he grabbed a 7,000-volt power line while climbing on a roof. Since then, he has used artificial arms and hooks for hands.

He took up golf in 1986, using special rubber bands to help him clasp the club. "At first it was frustrating," he told reporters. "Imagine trying to hold a golf club and not feel it, then swing your whole upper body to force the club in an arc. My friends said I should find an easier game. But I've never been a quitter and I vowed to play, arms or no arms."

Three years later, at the Golf Green Golf Center in Longview, Washington, Taylor drained his first ace. "I never thought I would see a hole in one in my life—and now I'd shot one with hooks instead of hands," he said. "When I got back to the clubhouse, the word had spread and I became an instant local celebrity."

Since then, Taylor has knocked in seven more aces, confirmed Skip Manke, the pro at the golf center. "Jim plays a great game of golf," said Manke. "He just happens to have no arms."

Most Unofficial Aces Scored in One Day

2 unofficial aces
John Murphy, 1982
Wil-Mar Golf Club
Raleigh, North Carolina

It was as though it had never happened.

In one memorable day, amateur John Murphy knocked two tee shots into the cup. But as far as the official rules of golf are concerned, he didn't score an ace either time.

The rules state that for a hole in one to be official, the shot must be witnessed by someone other than the golfer who made it. And it must come during an 18-hole round.

While playing a round by himself one day in 1982 at the Wil-Mar Golf Club, Murphy holed his tee shot at the 175-yard fifth hole. But because he was alone, Murphy knew the unwitnessed ace was not official.

So after he finished the round, Murphy recounted his bittersweet feat to Wil-Mar assistant greens superintendent Hank Grady and then took him back out to the fifth hole. There, the golfer put his tee into the ground and tried to demonstrate what had happened a few hours earlier.

Wonder of wonders, the ball landed in the cup again! But Murphy's joy was short-lived when he realized that this ace wasn't official either because he had played only one hole, and there wasn't enough time to complete a full round.

5

Wild Betting
Records

Most Pros Photographed Dropping Their Pants at the Same Time

4 pros
Jack Nicklaus, Arnold Palmer, Gay Brewer, Dave Hill
1973 Ryder Cup

It's one of the most treasured photographs in golf. Nicklaus, Palmer, Brewer, and Hill—all members of the 1973 U.S. Ryder Cup team—had their posteriors snapped for posterity.

It was all the result of a boast made by teammate Lee Trevino. Before his match on the Ryder Cup's final day against Peter Oosterhuis—the number-one player on the European Tour and the favorite—Trevino pledged, "If I don't beat that Peter Oosterhuis, I'll kiss the rears of every member of the team."

Unfortunately, Trevino didn't win. He and Oosterhuis halved the match. But the Americans won the Cup anyway, 19–13, so they were in a mischievous mood when they all convened in the locker room at Scotland's Muirfield Golf Club.

One by one, they challenged Trevino to carry out his promise. They even brought in a photographer to record the event. The photo, guarded now in a private collection, shows Trevino seated, doubled up in laughter.

Nicklaus is removing his pants. Next to him is Palmer, doing the same thing. Brewer, wearing the team blazer, has already doffed his trousers, daring Trevino to pucker up. Dave Hill also has dropped trou.

Did Trevino ever follow through on his pledge? You can't tell from the picture . . . and, publicly, he won't tell anyone.

Fewest Shots Made to Reach a Target Three Miles Away

32
Freddie Tait, 1898
England

Freddie Tait, Scotland's premier golfer at the turn of the century, bet friends he could play from the clubhouse at England's Royal St. George's Golf Course to the one at Royal Cinque Ports Golf Club—a distance of three miles—in 40 shots or less.

There were two conditions. He could tee each shot, but he had to use a gutta percha. The gutty—fashioned out of a gummy substance from India with a hard billiard ball–like cover—was not known for its distance.

Nevertheless, Tait succeeded in dramatic fashion. He reached the grounds of Cinque Ports in only 31 strokes and let fly with his 32nd shot directly at the clubhouse. The ball shattered a window, signaling Tait the winner of the bet.

Most Money Won by a Pro for Biting the Cover off a Golf Ball

$50
Andy Bean, 1974–present

Andy Bean will bite the cover off a golf ball for a $50 wager—or for laughs.

The first time he did it, though, was out of sheer exasperation.

In 1974, Bean, playing for the University of Florida, was paired against Wake Forest All-American Jay Haas in a big collegiate event. Bean had been nearly flawless all day, hitting every green in regulation on the first 17 holes.

He was 2 under par as he stood behind his four-foot birdie putt on the final hole, waiting for Haas to try a 30-footer. Haas had hit only 11 greens in regulation but he had scrambled well all day and actually led in the match with a score of three under par. However, if Bean made his birdie and Haas two-putted as expected from long range, the match would end in a tie.

But to Bean's shock, Haas holed his long putt for a birdie. A shaken Bean then missed his shortie.

Bean was so angry that he shoved his golf ball between his teeth and chomped on it with all his might. To everyone's amazement, the cover split and a chunk of the insides flew out of his mouth. Bean then spit out the split ball and flung it into the nearby bushes.

"I didn't think anything about it," Bean recalled. "But Jay jumped in those bushes and got the ball. For the rest of the day, he showed it to everybody. He just couldn't believe it."

Bean says he can still bite a chunk out of the cover of a new Titleist, but he hasn't been that angry on the course in years. However, Bean says, he has won several bets with friends, fans, and fellow golfers foolish enough to wager $50 that he can't do it.

Most Money Lost on a Calcutta Auction at the U.S. Amateur

$23,000
Henry Lapham, 1929
Pebble Beach

Bobby Jones was an overwhelming favorite to win the 1929 U.S. Amateur at Pebble Beach, the first major event ever held at the storied course.

In the opening round of match play, Jones, who already had won three U.S. Opens and two British Opens, was pitted against Johnny Goodman, a 19-year-old unknown from Omaha. Virtually no one in California had heard of Goodman, including Henry Lapham, a wealthy San Franciscan who had purchased Jones in a Calcutta auction the night before the tournament.

In a Calcutta, club members bid for the golfer they think will win. The high bidder for each player "buys" him. The buyer of the golfer who wins the tournament collects the money from the high bidders of each of the other players.

Thinking he had a sure bet, Lapham bought Jones for the then unheard-of price of $23,000 (equivalent to $250,000 today). But to everyone's shock—especially Lapham's—Jones fell behind Goodman quickly, losing the first three holes. He battled back, though, to win the next two holes and evened the match after 13 holes. But Jones bogeyed the 14th to give Goodman a one-hole lead and they halved the 15th, 16th, and 17th.

Jones had a chance to tie Goodman on the final hole, but his putt for birdie stopped six inches wide of the hole. Although he had played the round a stroke lower than Goodman, Jones was out of the tournament because he had lost in match play. But the person who suffered most by the stunning defeat was Henry Lapham. He was out $23,000.

Fastest Round in Dense Fog Without Losing a Ball

2 hours, 15 minutes
John Ball, 1907
Hoylake Golf Course
England

John Ball, England's leading amateur player at the time, arrived at Hoylake near Liverpool one day when fog made it impossible to see the flagstick from the edge of the green.

Other golfers decided it wasn't worth the hassle of hunting all day for golf balls in the thick soup. Ball contended they were wimps. So one of them presented him with a sporting wager that he quickly accepted.

To win the bet, Ball had to play 18 holes at Hoylake in less than 2½ hours, break 90, and play the entire round with the same ball.

He won the bet, zipping around the fog-shrouded course in 2 hours, 15 minutes, and shooting an 81. And he did it without losing a ball. That's because before teeing off, he had painted his ball black!

Lowest Score Shot by a Golfer Who Predicted the Results

64
Joe Ezar, 1936
Sestriere Golf Club
Sestriere, Italy

Joe Ezar, one of the game's most colorful hustlers and trick shot artists, won a hefty wager when he broke a course record just as he predicted he would.

In the town of Sestriere, site of the Italian Open the following week, Ezar met the president of the Fiat Motor Company on the golf course. The two were exchanging boasts about their linksmanship when Ezar claimed he could tie the course record of 66 the next day.

"I'll bet you 5,000 lira that you can't match it," said the auto bigwig.

"And if I break the record with a 65?" asked Ezar.

"I'll double it."

"And how much would a score of 64 be worth?" the golfer queried.

"Forty thousand lira," came the reply.

"I'll tell you what I'll do," Ezar said. "Before I play the round, I'll write down the score I'll make on each hole for my 64."

After jotting down his hole-by-hole predictions, Ezar headed straight to the bar where he drank away most of the night. Were it not for a very persistent caddie who dragged him out of bed the next morning, the besotted Ezar would never even have made it to the course.

With a camel hair coat draped around his shoulders, Ezar staggered to the first tee. Despite bleary eyes, shaky hands, and wobbly legs, he golfed with the consummate skill of a Bobby Jones. Incredibly, Ezar played the first eight holes exactly as he had predicted.

He slipped on the ninth hole, making a 4 where he had predicted a 3. But he made up for it on the next hole by sinking a birdie putt for a 3 instead of the 4 he had forecast.

Ezar then matched his predicted scores for the last eight holes and broke the course record by shooting a 64—just as he said he would.

The hung-over hustler pocketed the 40,000 lira and promptly went back to the bar to celebrate.

Most Strokes an Amateur Gave a U.S. Open Champion in a Round

2 strokes
Bobby Jones, 1928

Tommy Armour won the U.S. Open at Oakmont Country Club near Pittsburgh in 1927—a tournament where the legendary Bobby Jones played poorly. Jones finished in a tie for 11th, unthinkable for him in that era. But both golfers knew that Jones was the better player.

In the summer that followed, Armour and Jones, who were close friends, played numerous friendly matches for small wagers. Armour never won.

Jones was embarrassed by taking money from a professional whose friendship he valued so highly. So he began discreetly giving Armour strokes in their matches—one a side.

Jones's sporting gesture would never have been known had not Armour himself told the story later in life. Jones never mentioned it to a soul, but Armour had no problem confessing that he couldn't beat Jones without an "equalizer."

Asked how a Tour pro could accept "ups" from an amateur, particularly when the pro was the reigning U.S. Open champion at the time, Armour bristled, "because that's how goddamn good Bobby was."

Most Money Won on the Golf Course by an Army Private While Trying to Get Home

$45
Chi Chi Rodriguez, 1959
Fort Dix Golf Course
Fort Dix, New Jersey

While Chi Chi Rodriguez was in special services in the Army, he won the post's golf championship at Fort Sill, Oklahoma. By the time he was due to be discharged, his golf game was nearing Tour caliber.

Chi Chi was sent to Fort Dix, New Jersey, for the official mustering out. He hoped to fly home to Puerto Rico, but there was this rather urgent matter of funds. He only had $45 in his pocket and the plane ticket cost $55.

He wandered over to the golf course, where he knew he might be able to hustle enough money to buy a ticket home. By chance, the Fort Dix post champion was on the course and Chi Chi talked him into a friendly wager.

"I told him I'd stand on my head, and whatever fell out of my pockets, I'd play for," Chi Chi recalled. "I needed $55 dollars for the plane fare. He was a sergeant and I was a PFC weighing 117 pounds. If I lost, I would have had to stay on the base and pull kitchen duty for who knows how long."

Needing desperately to win so he could go home, Rodriguez played one of his best games up to then. "I birdied the first five holes and won," he said. "I collected my money and made the plane."

Lowest Score Ever Shot by a Pro to Win a Bet

57
Orville Moody, 1979
Bowie Country Club
San Antonio, Texas

In 1979, pro Orville Moody wound up in a small-stakes gambling match with some of the locals at San Antonio's Bowie Country Club. He proceeded to have one of the best golfing days of his life, shooting a stunning 57.

"The course was only about 6,300 yards [in length]," he recalled. "But I made three eagles. Hey, you've got to hit some good shots to shoot 57 on a par-72 course. I don't care how short it is."

When the round was over, some of the skeptics told Moody that he really wasn't that good. They said it was a fluke or pure luck. It was, they contended, something besides just incredible talent.

Moody listened for a while, then got fed up with them. "Let's go back out," he said, "and I'll show you again." And that's exactly what he did. He tore through the front nine in 30. The naysayers were convinced. End of round.

For 27 holes on that remarkable day, Moody shot an amazing 87.

Lowest Nine-Hole Score for a Blindfolded Golfer Using Only a 5-Iron, an 8-Iron, and a Putter

46
Jim England, 1976
Chapparal Country Club
Bullhead City, Arizona

Jim England, of Bullhead City, Arizona, played a round that made him wonder why he ever used a full bag of clubs.

Recalled his wife, Mary, "Fortified with a good supply of confidence-building joy juice, my husband bet some friends he could break 50 on the front side of Chapparal Country Club, using only a 5-iron, 8-iron, and putter. And furthermore, he would hit every shot blindfolded."

So his blindman's bluff was called and he went out to the course with the three clubs and a blindfold. To everyone's amazement, England broke 50 by four strokes, shooting a 46.

The next day, still savoring his victory and counting his modest winnings, he played the front nine again. This time, he had all 14 clubs in his bag and hit all his shots without a blindfold.

He shot a 48!

Most Money Won by a Pro Betting on a Fellow Competitor

$60,000
Bobby Cruickshank, 1930

In 1930, Bobby Jones was the golfing rage of the American sporting public. One of his biggest fans was fellow competitor Bobby Cruickshank.

Like almost every pro golfer, Cruickshank knew that Jones, who maintained his amateur status throughout his playing days, was in a class by himself. Figuring he could never beat Jones, Cruickshank hoped to make money on Jones's victories.

Before the golf season, bookies announced that as great a player as Jones was, they didn't think it was likely that he would win all four majors. Back then, the Grand Slam included the U.S. Open, U.S. Amateur, British Open, and British Amateur. Bookies offered odds of a Jones Grand Slam at 120 to 1.

Cruickshank was so sure Jones would win it all that he wagered $500. Jones proceeded to capture all four majors. While Jones declined to accept any prize winnings, Cruickshank came away with the big bucks, happily pocketing $60,000.

79

Lowest Score Playing St. Andrews by the Light of the Moon

93
Dave Struth, 1876

Well-known Scottish golfer David Struth bet friends that he could play St. Andrews in less than 100 strokes—at night under a full moon.

He beat his goal by seven shots. And, amazingly, he shot his 93 without losing a ball.

6

Zany
Rules Infractions

Most Penalty Strokes Caused by a
Four-Year-Old

4 penalty strokes
Dustin Eggeling
1992 JC Penney Classic

Four-year-old Dustin Eggeling had no idea of the
chaos he would cause when he stuffed his own little
cut-down 7-iron into the golf bag of his mother, pro
golfer Dale Eggeling.

It seemed innocent enough. After all, that's
where Mom put her clubs. The problem was that
Eggeling didn't know her son's club was in her bag.

She discovered it at the worst possible time—in
the middle of a tournament. At the JC Penney Classic
in Tarpon Springs, Florida, Eggeling hit a shot on the
15th hole and handed her club to her caddie, who
nonchalantly slipped it into the bag. When it
wouldn't slide to the bottom, the caddie peered inside and was horrified to see the tiny club jammed in
the bottom. Golf rules allow only 14 clubs, and Dustin's 7-iron put Dale over the limit at 15.

A penalty was in order, despite the absurdity of
the situation. The rules state that two strokes must be
added for every hole the bag is over the limit, with a
maximum of four strokes. At the end of the day in the
mixed team event, the score of Eggeling and her
playing partner, Wayne Levi, zoomed from a 74 to a
78. They finished in 60th place.

"It's apparent that, at some time, Dustin was playing and stuck it in my bag," Eggeling said. "I didn't
check. I just screwed up."

A similar incident had happened to Nancy Lopez
earlier in the year when she discovered one of her
children's toy clubs in her bag during an LPGA tournament. Fortunately for Lopez, she wasn't penalized

because the club was plastic and not an official club. Unfortunately for Eggeling, Dustin's cut-down 7-iron fit the definition of a golf club, since it had a definable head and a metal shaft.

Most Severe Penalty Assessed for Being Addicted to Golf

Beheading
Mary, Queen of Scots, 1587

Because of her consuming passion for golf, Mary, Queen of Scots, singlehandedly raised the game's popularity to new heights. Yet, ironically, golf was her downfall and led to her eventual execution.

Scotland—the cradle of golf—actually had banned the sport. In March 1457, King James II decreed "that golf be utterly cryed downe and not used." He was concerned that the Scots, who were constantly battling the English, were devoting too much attention to golf at the expense of archery and, thus, national defense.

A century later, Mary brought golf back into favor in Scotland after she became quite smitten with the game, ironically, in France. When she returned to her homeland after the death of her first husband, Francis, in 1565, the Queen raised plenty of eyebrows. She ignored affairs of state and instead headed out to the links with sons of French nobles serving as her caddies.

Her passion for golf was matched only by her passion for men. After she wed her second husband, Lord Darnley, Mary continued to score on the fairways while her philandering hubby scored in the boudoirs of other women. Because of his constant romantic soirees, Mary found another paramour, who happened to like golf. But a jealous Darnley murdered the Queen's lover.

A short time later, Lord Darnley died in a massive explosion at his home. However, when experts inspected his body, they discovered he had been strangled.

Mary became a suspect, especially when the not-so-grieving widow interrupted her mourning just days after her husband's death to get in a few rounds of golf. Scottish Presbyterians were outraged, and became even more so three months later when Mary wed the Earl of Bothwell. Her shocked subjects felt the Queen had recovered much too quickly from her sorrow.

In 1567 the country's best-known golfer was forced to abdicate her throne. Even worse, she was put on trial for treason in England by Elizabeth I, never known for her fondness for golf. Mary's rounds of golf after Darnley's death were recounted as evidence of her ruthless coldheartedness. She was convicted and then beheaded.

At least Mary made the cut.

Costliest Fine for a Pro Repeating His Favorite Swear Words

$1,000
Ken Green
1991 JC Penney Classic

Pro Ken Green, known for having an extremely colorful vocabulary, discovered it doesn't pay to talk dirty even in jest. In fact, it can be downright costly.

In 1991, Green was playing in the JC Penney

Classic, a mixed team event, with LPGA pro Barb Bunkowsky. In the interview room at Innisbrook Resort in Tarpon Springs, Florida, Green was in a joking mood and talked to reporters about Bunkowsky, who refuses to utter four-letter words. "Being a Christian, she doesn't swear, so I get to swear twice as much—after my shots and hers," Green joked with reporters.

Green explained then that his two favorite epithets on the course were "shit" and "fuck," and then, to underscore his feelings about those words, he repeated them several times.

Once was too many for Connie Wilson of the LPGA media staff. She reported Green's dissertation on obscenities to the PGA Tour office. After a quick investigation, Green was slapped with a $1,000 fine.

"I was kidding around and explaining my theories on those two words," Green said later. "The fine did surprise me. I can understand if I get caught saying it on the golf course and it comes over the tube. Maybe it's a bad habit.

"But there are a lot of bad habits. Smoking is a bad habit, but we're allowed to smoke. Smoking will kill you. Swearing can't."

Biggest Fine for Embarrassing the Tournament Hosts

$475
Mark James
1978 French Open

English pro Mark James thought he'd have a little fun at the final ceremonies of the French Open. With the gallery looking on, officials handed out pay envelopes to the top finishers.

James, who had finished fifth at the European Tour event and won $3,230, opened his envelope with a flourish, then feigned shock when he saw nothing was inside. He showed the empty envelope to the spectators, who laughed heartily.

Tournament officials, however, failed to see the humor. James was fined $475 for "behavior in poor taste."

Explained Ken Schofield, who at the time was secretary of the European Tour, "Everybody on the Tour knows it is the custom to pay the money in sterling the following day." The passing out of pay envelopes to the golfers was for the benefit of the gallery, who weren't supposed to know the envelopes were empty. "That fact was well known to James," added Schofield.

That wasn't the only time James was fined by the Tour. He was assessed a $100 fine for throwing his putter into a tree. "My putter wasn't working and I had had enough of it," James explained. "So I threw it away. I aimed at a lake but it hit the tree."

Most Penalty Strokes for Playing Too Fast

2 penalty strokes
Donnie Hammond
1983 Bay Hill Classic

Donnie Hammond learned the hard way how costly it is to play too fast.

Hammond was playing in his first Bay Hill Classic, in a star-studded pairing that included Jack Nicklaus and David Graham. At the nine-hole turn, Nicklaus ducked into the locker room to relieve himself while Hammond and Graham proceeded onto the 10th tee.

Hammond had shot the front side in only 32 strokes and wasn't anxious to break his rhythm with a lengthy delay. It was Nicklaus's honor on the tee, but the Golden Bear was nowhere in sight.

"After waiting a few minutes, David told me to go ahead and hit so we could get moving," Hammond recalled. "So I did with a drive right in the middle of the fairway. Then he hit, too. We started walking down the fairway when Jack finally showed up."

Nicklaus hit his drive and caught up with Hammond, who wasn't yet an official member of the PGA Tour. Hammond knew something was wrong when Nicklaus put his arm around him. "He told me, 'Donnie, I think we've got a problem,' " Hammond related. " 'I think you're going to have to add two strokes to your score. I'm afraid the rules say we had to play in order.' "

Sure enough, Hammond was assessed the strokes at the end of the round. Graham, though, was spared any penalty because the rule at the time only penalized the first person to hit out of turn. It wouldn't have been a penalty had Hammond hit out of turn by mistake. But because he did it deliberately, he was penalized.

The infraction didn't much matter to Hammond. He shot a horrendous 48 on the back nine and finished in a tie for 40th place.

Longest March by GIs for Insulting Women Golfers

15 miles
Soldiers of the Second Army, 1955
Memphis Country Club
Memphis, Tennessee

Hundreds of GIs from the Second Army learned a lesson in golf etiquette that they would never forget.

The soldiers were in a 45-vehicle convoy heading to maneuvers at Camp Robinson, Arkansas, when they rolled past the Memphis Country Club and spotted two women golfing on the course. Like typical jerks in the days before sexual harassment was even a term, the GIs let loose with a chorus of lusty catcalls such as: "Yoo hoo!" "Fore—play!" "Keep your head down—in my lap!" After the trucks passed, the soldiers hunkered back down in their seats and forgot about the incident.

But General Ben Lear didn't. General Lear was the commander of the Second Army and, by a stroke of luck, had been playing the course as his troops rode by. He heard every one of their crass shouts at the women.

While the convoy proceeded to its destination, General Lear finished his round. Then he phoned Camp Robinson and ordered the soldiers to return to Memphis immediately.

After the convoy retraced the entire 140-mile route, the soldiers dismounted, stood at attention, and listened to a stern lecture from General Lear on golf course etiquette and respect for women.

Then he ordered the GIs to head back to Camp Robinson. But the general made them march the first

15 miles of the journey—which took them past the country club where they had shouted their sexist yells.

To the soldiers who were forced to walk it, the hike was forever known as the "Yoo-Hoo March."

Costliest Mistake by a Tour Pro Caddying for a Friend

2-stroke penalty
Fred Couples
1988 K Mart Greater Greensboro Open

On the Monday preceding the K Mart Greater Greensboro Open, Fred Couples found himself in town with nothing to do. Then he learned that his friend Tom Patri was scheduled to play in the qualifier for one of the four open spots in the tournament.

So Couples volunteered to carry his pal's bag, and Patri readily accepted the help. All went well until the ninth hole after Patri yanked his drive into the rough. Couples dutifully trudged after the ball and found it in the high grass. He then dropped the bag and watched Patri play the shot to the green.

The two had walked only a few feet when they spotted another ball. Fearing the worst, they looked it over—and sure enough, it was Patri's. Couples had made a caddie's worst error, identifying a lost ball as his player's when it really wasn't.

Patri had to take a two-stroke penalty and replay the shot. As a result, he did not make the field for the tournament, missing out on a chance to win some money.

Worst Score of a Hole Halved by Penalty Strokes

Double bogey
John Flannery and Esteban Toledo
1991 Ben Hogan Reno Open

John Flannery and Esteban Toledo ran afoul of the Rules of Golf, triggering the most bizarre finish in Hogan Tour history.

They were locked in a sudden-death playoff at the Ben Hogan Reno Open at Northgate Country Club. On the third extra hole, Flannery marked his ball on the green before attempting a par putt. He was in Toledo's line, so he moved his mark a putter-head length away. Toledo then missed his par putt.

Moments later, Flannery made his putt for what appeared to be a par and the victory. Toledo's caddie then picked up Toledo's marker, figuring that holing out was useless since the playoff was over.

But wait! Flannery had not replaced his ball at the site of the original mark. He forgot that he had moved out of the way of Toledo's putt. Flannery was slapped with a two-stroke penalty, giving him a double bogey.

But Toledo couldn't be declared the winner because he didn't hole out after his caddie picked up his mark. For not properly finishing the hole, Toledo was penalized one stroke. So he, too, scored a double bogey.

As a result, the hole was halved with double bogeys!

However, Flannery's brain sprain didn't cost him the tourney. On the next hole, he made a penalty-free par for the victory.

Most Spirited Fine for Not Wearing the Club Uniform

Six pints of ale
James Dalrymple, 1776
Leith Golf Club
Scotland

Back in the 18th century, it was a serious matter to play at the Leith Golf Club without wearing the official uniform of a red jacket (with the club's crest), a black tie, a white shirt, and beige knickers.

Lieutenant James Dalrymple would find out just how serious when he repeatedly breached the decorum at the Scottish club by playing without his jacket and tie. The Honourable Company of Edinburgh golfers finally had no choice but to take him to task for his repeated oversights.

The club minutes of November 16, 1776, report that the lieutenant was found guilty of playing five times without the requisite wardrobe. His fine was to pay for six pints of ale, presumably downed by those who sat in judgment.

Costliest Penalty for Moving a Boundary Stake

$81,563
Chip Beck
1992 Greater Greensboro Open

In the third round of the Greater Greensboro Open, Chip Beck yanked his tee shot on the 15th hole and watched helplessly as it landed next to an out-of-bounds marker.

When Beck, who was tied for the lead at the time, lined up his next shot, he pulled the stake out of the ground. As he stood there with the marker in his hand, he realized that he might be violating a rule. So he stuck it back into its original position and played the shot.

Alas, it was too late. The act of simply removing the boundary stake, even though he replaced it before hitting his shot, constituted a two-stroke penalty. Those two extra strokes gave him a triple bogey for the hole.

How costly was the infraction? Beck finished in a tie for third in the tournament and earned $53,437. Had he not fiddled with the boundary stake, he would have finished all alone in second place. That would have given him a check for $135,000—a difference of $81,563.

Stiffest Penalty for a Tour Pro Winning a Dinner Bet

One year's probation
Al Besselink
1965 San Diego Open

Al Besselink was a loosey-goosey kind of pro who loved a good wager—even during a PGA event.

Chatting with a friend moments before the first round of the San Diego Open, Besselink told him, "I'll bet you I can break 67 today."

"You're on," said the friend. "Loser buys dinner."

"Nah," retorted Besselink. "Let's really stack the odds in your favor. I'll bet you 10 dinners against your one dinner that I can do it."

For a while it looked like Besselink was going to

be springing for plenty of dinner checks. He started out with five consecutive pars. At the sixth hole, though, Besselink finally nailed a birdie and went on a hot streak. By the time he reached the 18th hole, he needed only to make a par to score 66 and win the bet. Besselink did one better by sinking a 20-foot putt for birdie and a score of 65.

The next day the *San Diego Union* carried a light-hearted story about the wager. But PGA tournament director Jim Gaquin didn't find it funny. He slapped Besselink with a one-year probation. "Besselink lives in one world, we live in another," Gaquin told the press. "We can't allow gambling during regular competition. We'll never try to control $5 Nassaus during practice rounds, but the PGA must retain dignity and respect in the public's eye. Many of the players were upset when Al's gambling hit the press."

Besselink had his own version of why some of his fellow golfers were angry at him. "They didn't like it because I blabbed to the press," he said. "I'm in the limelight, that's all. I guess they thought they had to do something."

Largest Fine in LPGA History

$3,500
Lori Garbacz
1985 LPGA National Pro-Am

Lori Garbacz, one of the most emotional players on the LPGA Tour, holds the record for the stiffest fine ever given a lady pro. At the 1985 LPGA National Pro-Am, she let loose with an obscenity-spiced outburst that was broadcast live on television.

It happened during the third round of the tournament at Denver when Garbacz was protecting her shrinking lead. She had just bogeyed the 15th hole and double-bogeyed the 16th.

A cameraman from ESPN, which was televising the tournament, followed the golfer from the green to the next tee. As Garbacz stood waiting to hit her drive on the 17th, the cameraman continued to crowd her, waiting to get a reaction shot.

Suddenly Garbacz turned and gave him a reaction he'll never forget. "Get that fucking thing out of my face! Do you hear me?" she hollered in exasperation. Every word of her outburst was heard by the nationwide TV audience.

Although she later apologized to golf fans and her fellow pros for "unprofessional behavior," Garbacz was fined a record $3,500 by the LPGA.

Garbacz later explained that she didn't realize the microphone was on and called the tantrum "inadvertent." She added, however, that "it wasn't all my fault. He [the cameraman] should have known better than that. Sometimes I think TV has gone too far with the hand-held camera invading your privacy. I didn't ask him to come there and stick it in my face after a double bogey. I wanted to be myself and get my stuff together for the last two holes."

Largest Fine for Throwing a Ball Out of a Bunker

$500
Dave Hill
1971 Colonial Invitational

Dave Hill, one of the most temperamental golfers in Tour history, was having a rough day at the Colonial

Invitational in Fort Worth, Texas. His shots were going everywhere but where he wanted them to go.

On the 12th hole, his ball landed in yet another bunker. A steaming-mad Hill tromped into the bunker, gave his ball a sneer, then stunned everyone when he bent over and picked it up. The gallery was even more shocked when he tossed the ball like a hook shot in basketball toward the hole.

A thoroughly confused woman scorer, bumbling in awkwardness at the incident, asked Hill what score she should give him for the hole. "Just give me a two," Hill replied, "although I didn't make the basket."

The scorer did as Hill said, realizing that the golfer's round had now become a farce. At the end of the day, Hill compounded the folly by signing his obviously incorrect scorecard. As a result, Hill was summarily disqualified. The disqualification didn't bother him at all because he was playing poorly and wanted out of the event anyway.

In the locker room, Hill told reporters, "I always wanted to try throwing the ball at a hole. I thought I'd give it a try at the Colonial." PGA officials weren't amused and fined Hill $500 for conduct unbecoming a pro.

Biggest Penalty for Playing in a Tournament Without Permission

$500 fine, suspension from the PGA Tour, and removal from the Ryder Cup team
Sam Snead, 1961

A round of golf cost Sam Snead dearly.

After being chosen for the Ryder Cup team for

the 10th time, Snead was fitted for the team uniform and given a travel itinerary to Royal Lytham and St. Anne's in England for the matches.

Because he had played a busy schedule, Snead decided to take some time off before heading overseas. So he wrote to officials of the Portland Open, where he had committed to play, and informed them he wouldn't be participating. That same week, however, he suddenly decided to play in a pro-am in Cincinnati.

He was about to tee off in the event when he learned he might be in violation of a PGA rule. The tour prohibited pros from playing in an event at the same time a sanctioned tournament was in progress. Snead would have to get special permission to play in Cincinnati.

So Sam sent a telegram seeking an official release from his Portland obligation, then played his round. When he finished, he was chagrined to hear the return message from the PGA—permission had been denied.

Realizing he had broken the rule, Snead immediately withdrew from the Cincinnati event, hoping the PGA board would be sympathetic. The officials were not impressed, slapping him with a stiff penalty: a $500 fine and suspension from the PGA Tour for six months. Unfortunately, the dates of the Ryder Cup fell during that six-month period.

Snead filed an appeal, but it was not heard by the PGA until after the Ryder Cup. Thus, he couldn't play in the international event. However, Snead did win a minor victory. His suspension was reduced from six months to 45 days.

The U.S. Ryder Cup team got by nicely without him. With Arnold Palmer playing for the first time, the Americans won by a score of 14½ to 9½.

Most Expensive Shorts Worn by a Pro at a Tournament

$500 shorts
Mark Wiebe
1992 Anheuser-Busch Classic

The PGA Tour has a long-standing prohibition against wearing shorts in an official event, reasoning that regulation long pants preserve golf's status as a true "gentleman's game." And despite the efforts of such notables as Jack Nicklaus to modify the rule, PGA officials have stood firm.

When the temperature reached 102°F at the 1992 Anheuser-Busch Classic at Kingsmill Golf Club in Williamsburg, Virginia, Tour pro Mark Wiebe thought it was too hot to wear long pants. Rule or no rule, he decided comfort was more important than tradition. So he donned some shorts and went to the practice tee.

For giving the rule such short shrift, Wiebe was fined $500.

7

Crazy Equipment Records

Longest Time a Pro Carried an Out-of-Bounds Stake on Tour

6 months
Roger Maltbie, 1976

Roger Maltbie carried a wooden stake with him on the Tour for six months—not as a weapon against vampires but as a testament to Divine Providence.

Maltbie kept the old, white out-of-bounds marker in his bag because it was an ever-present reminder of a lucky shot that had helped him win the 1976 Memorial Tournament at Muirfield Village in Dublin, Ohio.

Maltbie and Hale Irwin were tied after the regulation 72 holes. During their playoff, Maltbie whacked a tee shot that was headed off the course until, in a remarkable stroke of good fortune, it plunked into the out-of-bounds stake. The ball caromed back toward the fairway, staying in fair territory. Maltbie parred the hole and went on to beat Irwin on the fourth playoff hole.

Overjoyed by his lucky victory, Maltbie pulled up the stake and triumphantly carried it out of Muirfield with him. "I never would have won if it hadn't been for the placement of that stake," Maltbie admitted. "This is my lucky charm." For the remainder of the year, he carried it with him on his stops around the Tour. One day, after a particularly poor performance on the links, he left the stake under his bed in a motel room.

Longest Time Stuck Up a Tree While Trying to Recover a Club

45 minutes
Bobby Knight, 1982
Indiana University Golf Course
Bloomington, Indiana

Indiana University's Bobby Knight plays golf the way he coaches basketball—hurling angry Anglo-Saxon curses as well as anything he can get his hands on. Because of his volatile temper, he has occasionally stormed off the links—and once was stuck up a tree.

One day, while playing on the school's course, Knight missed an easy, short putt on the fifth hole. The putter, being the only thing in his hand, was in trouble. "I tossed it in the air and it hung up in a tree," he confessed to *Golf* magazine years later.

He flung his club so high that it disappeared in a fully grown maple, which promptly gobbled up the putter and refused to drop it. So Knight went stalking off to the next hole.

The following day, Knight had forgiven the offending club. "I wanted it back," he said. "So I went out there by myself and climbed the tree."

First, though, he made sure no one saw him by hustling to the fifth green early in the morning before any golfers had reached the fifth tee. Lifting himself up from branch to branch, Knight found himself 40 feet off the ground, but he still couldn't reach his putter. The coach was experiencing mixed emotions—impressed that he could toss a putter that high up into a tree and peeved that he couldn't retrieve it.

Rather than risk serious injury by going any higher, Knight decided that the putter wasn't all that good anyway and probably would have caused him nothing but more anguish. He was all set to ease his way down the tree when he encountered a new problem.

Golfers had already reached the fifth hole. As a well-known figure on the Indiana campus, Knight couldn't just plop down from a tree. The golfers would instantly recognize him and confirm the assumption that so many already have of the coach—that he's not playing with all his clubs.

So, crouched quietly on a branch high in the maple tree, Knight waited for the group to hole out. But then moments later, another foursome landed their approach shots. So Knight had to remain up in the tree. In fact, he was stuck up there for 45 minutes. Recalled the coach, "I had to wait for four groups to play through before I could come down."

Most Golf Shoes Stolen by a Dog

2 golf shoes
Black Labrador, 1984
Brightondale Park Golf Course
Kansasville, Wisconsin

Before heading onto the links at the Brightondale Park Golf Course, Tom Noonan of nearby Lake Geneva left his golf shoes and bag outside the clubhouse for a few minutes. But when he returned, his shoes were missing.

After asking fellow golfers if they had seen who had swiped his shoes, Noonan found a witness who claimed the culprit was a black Labrador. The dog had picked up one of the shoes, carried it off into the nearby woods, and then come back for the other. A search of the area failed to turn up the shoes or the dog.

"I'd worn those shoes only three times," lamented Noonan. "They cost me sixty bucks—and I'll bet that dog never wore them."

Most Rounds a Pro Played with the Same Ball

4 rounds
Sam Snead
1945 Los Angeles Open

Sam Snead had long held the reputation as one of golf's tightwads, but he outdid himself at the 1945 Los Angeles Open. In an era when golf balls weren't nearly as durable as they are now, Snead played the entire tournament with just one ball!

Actually, he didn't have much choice. It was wartime, there was a national rubber shortage, and golf balls had become very expensive, even for the big spenders who had much looser purse strings than Snead.

"You couldn't get balls then," Snead explained later. "I was paying $100 a dozen. Bing Crosby gave me a ball, a Spalding Dot, and I played it throughout the tournament. The cover was loose, but it kept going."

Incredibly, the ball held up long enough for Slammin' Sam to win the tournament!

Most Times Using a Driver on One Hole to Score a Birdie

3 times
Thomas Dowd, 1978
Azalea Sands Golf Club
Myrtle Beach, South Carolina

Thomas Dowd of Bethesda, Maryland, hit a poor drive at Azalea Sands Golf Club's par-4, 367-yard 16th hole.

He still needed 220 yards to reach the cup. Since the ball was sitting up high enough in the grass, he decided to swat the driver again. This time, without the use of a tee, the ball took off magnificently, reaching the green and dying just eight feet from the hole.

Well, shoot, I've used the same club twice now and have gotten this close, Dowd thought. Why not give it one more try, and see if I can accomplish something really special—getting a birdie with every shot off a driver?

Dowd choked up on the driver, bent over, and rolled the ball into the cup for a birdie!

Most New Practice Balls Stolen by Golfers in a Tournament

1,008 new practice balls
1991 British Amateur

Golf is a gentleman's game, right?

Try telling that to the Royal and Ancient, the governing body of golf in Europe. The R&A discovered that golf can be a game of light-fingered players.

The R&A, trying to do something a little special for competitors at the 1991 British Amateur, provided 84 dozen just-out-of-the-box bright and shiny balata balls for the practice range. The R&A shelled out $44 a dozen, or $3,696 for 1,008 balata balls.

Apparently, the temptation by the tourney participants to swipe the balls was just too great. By the end of the British Amateur, all the balatas were gone—carried off by golfers who felt these balls were too good to be used on the practice range.

Most Heroic 2-Iron Shot Ever Made

Larry LeBoeuf, 1992
Ptarmigan Country Club
Fort Collins, Colorado

Larry LeBoeuf's best 2-iron shot ever had nothing to do with the ball he hit, but rather the club he *threw*.

While approaching the sixth hole at Ptarmigan Country Club, LeBoeuf and his pals saw an automobile pull up beside the green and a teenager hop out. While the golfers watched in disbelief, the teen grabbed the flagstick from the hole and then bolted back into the car, which squealed off at high speed.

Knowing the road doubled back alongside the seventh fairway, LeBoeuf yanked his 2-iron from his golf bag and dashed off in hot pursuit. He raced across the fairway, but getting to the road was another story. He had to plod through an eight-foot-wide creek, climb up an embankment, and then scramble through a barbed wire fence.

Just as LeBoeuf reached the road, he saw the car barreling toward him. With all the skill of an Australian boomerang tosser, LeBoeuf hurled his 2-iron at the car. His timing was perfect. The club ricocheted off the open passenger-side window and, incredibly, smacked into the flagstick, knocking it from the hands of the young thief. LeBoeuf then triumphantly retrieved the stolen pin and his trusty 2-iron.

It was no big deal, LeBoeuf told those who congratulated him. With tongue firmly planted in cheek, he said, "When you've had as much practice as I have in hitting the flagstick with a 2-iron, this isn't all that spectacular."

Highest Rate of Inflation of the Price of a Putter

$60 in four hours
Purchased by Gary Player, 1961
Tokyo, Japan

Gary Player and Arnold Palmer were in Tokyo in 1961 for the opening of a new golf course. The greens were slow, so Player went browsing in the pro shop for a putter that he thought would punch the ball a bit more briskly across the higher grass.

In a barrel of putters, Player found an elongated black blade that seemed just what he was looking for. It had enough loft, Player reasoned, to make the ball roll better on the slow greens. Best of all, it had a price tag that was the equivalent of only $5.

Player held the putter up for Palmer's approval. But Arnie shook his head and suggested that Player continue searching for a better putter.

So Player left the shop empty-handed. But he couldn't get his mind off the putter. So after playing a round with Palmer, he walked back into the shop to buy it.

Player was shocked to see a new price tag on the putter. A shop attendant had noticed the golfer's earlier interest in the club and decided that if it was that good a putter, then $5 was probably way too little to charge for it. Now, the putter had a new tag—$65.

Player protested over the price, but to no avail. Reluctantly, he paid the inflated cost.

Today, Player considers the $65 a bargain. He since has used the putter to win dozens of tournaments around the world, earning him millions of dollars.

Most Consecutive Rounds Played with the Same Ball

46 consecutive rounds
Judge Michael Nehemiah Manning, 1928–29
Taladega, Alabama

Judge Michael Nehemiah Manning didn't have to budget much money each year for golf balls.

Judge Manning purchased a Kro-Flite golf ball on November 15, 1928, and retired it on January 28, 1929, after using it to play 46 rounds of 18 holes each. His average score per round was 82, which means he whacked the ball approximately 2,000 times, exclusive of putts.

Whenever the ball sailed off the fairway, the judge pursued it with vigor. He and his playing partners would search among the weeds, many times taking more than the allotted five minutes to look for it.

Obviously, they don't make players—or golf balls—like they used to.

Most Expensive Set of Clubs Made from a Ship's Propeller

$16,500
From the Queen Elizabeth 2

Probably never in history have golf clubs been made from such an unlikely metal source. But when the world's last great Cunard ocean liner, the *Queen Elizabeth 2*, was refitted in 1986–87, its two original propellers were replaced.

Each propeller contained a massive amount of rare metal—32½ tons of a marine bronze alloy called Superston 70. The alloy offered both strength and the color of platinum, with a nice tinge of gold. The active minds at Sandhill Limited, a Yorkshire, England, precious metals company, proposed a great moneymaking idea. Why not melt the propellers down and turn them into golf clubs?

So the metal from the melted-down props was sent to the Swilken clubmakers at St. Andrews, Scotland. (Appropriately, the *Queen Elizabeth 2* was originally built and outfitted in Scotland.) Swilken craftspeople then fashioned the metal into golf sets, each priced at a whopping $16,500. Each set included three persimmon woods (1-3-5), 10 irons (1-SW), and a putter. That comes to $1,178.57 per club.

There were other goodies thrown in with the set—a leather bag, an umbrella, a shirt, a dozen balls, a towel, shoe bags, a ball marker, and even tees. Everything, incidentally, sported the *QE2* logo.

Most Lost Balls Found by a Pro Without Finding His Own

26 balls
Mark Brooks
1991 Las Vegas Invitational

Mark Brooks had some bad news, good news, and even more bad news during the Las Vegas Invitational.

The bad news was that he lost two balls. The good news was that he found 26 balls while looking for his lost ones. But the more bad news was that none of them were his!

After battling near the lead with excellent scores of 67 and 65, Brooks hit into trouble in the third round on the 17th hole when an errant shot lodged high in a palm tree.

A cherry picker was summoned to hoist Brooks up into the tree so he could try to locate his ball. He poked around through the fronds and gathered eight balls. But none were his, so he was forced to take a stroke-and-distance penalty. It cost him a double bogey and he finished the round with a 74.

The next day, Brooks suffered further misfortune, this time at the 18th hole. After placing his approach shot safely on the green, he marked his ball, picked it up, and tossed it to his caddie. But his caddie missed the ball. To their horror, the ball rolled into a greenside lake before it could be stopped.

The rules say a player will be penalized two strokes if he doesn't complete the hole with the same ball that he played off the tee. So Brooks took off his shoes and socks, rolled up his pants, and waded into the water. He fished around with his hands and his feet, eventually pulling up 18 balls. Alas, none were his. So once again he had to take two penalty strokes for a double bogey, giving him a 78 for the day.

For the tournament, Brooks found a total of 26 balls, all belonging to other unlucky golfers—but none as unlucky as he was.

Most Kids Scrambling to Swipe Tees at a Golfing Event

50 kids (estimated)
Walter Hagen and Joe Kirkwood exhibition,
1922
Shennecosset Club
Groton, Connecticut

Curiously enough, it wasn't the mere presence of the famed Walter Hagen and Australian traveling mate Joe Kirkwood that persuaded officials to rope off the crowds. What got out of hand was the uncontrollable scramble for the golfers' tees.

Hagen and Kirkwood were among the first pros ever to use wooden tees, which had just been invented. The golfers introduced them during an exhibition at the Shennecosset Club.

"Joe and I strutted around the course with the bright red tees stuck behind our ears," Hagen recalled. "At each tee we used them and left them. Kids scrambled onto the course, grabbing them as souvenirs. They became so popular that the club found it necessary to rope off the tees and fairways to control the galleries. This was the first time in U.S. golf history that gallery-control ropes were used."

The wooden tees revolutionized golf. For centuries, players hit their drives off earth-made tees fashioned from a handful of dirt. In 1921, Dr. William Lowell, a dentist from Maplewood, New Jersey, grew tired of coming home from a round of golf with dirty hands and clothes. So he whittled little pegs from a wooden flagpole in front of his home. Then he began mass-producing his tees, which he painted red and called Reddy Tees.

In 1922, he gave them to Hagen and Kirkwood to promote on their exhibition tour. By 1926 there were more than 200 different brands of tees marketed by competitors.

Most Range Balls Gobbled Up by Ice Plant

12,000 range balls
Corral de Tierra Country Club, 1980
Salinas, California

Harold Firstman, the pro at Corral de Tierra Country Club, had a mystery on his hands. His range balls were disappearing at an alarming rate, faster than anyone could possibly steal them.

Then he found the culprit. One day, while standing around the practice range watching club members hit balls, he noticed that some golfers were topping their shots into a stretch of turf covered with ice plant. That, he reasoned, might be where most of his range balls were.

Ice plant is a thick, rubbery plant with tentacles that hide the ground, making it practically impenetrable. A ball that rolls into it is often lost for good.

So Firstman hired a bulldozer operator to clear out the ice plant down to the bare earth. Sure enough, hidden by the vegetation sat about 12,000 balls!

"We won't have to buy any range balls for at least four years," said Firstman, who replanted the former ball trap—with grass.

Highest Percentage of Holes in One Made with One Club

1.000
Rick Pierce, 1992
Orlando, Florida

Rick Pierce, a time-share salesman from Orlando, has a 6-iron hanging over the mantel of his home because the club has achieved perfection. The first and only time Pierce ever swung it, he knocked the ball into the 15th hole at MetroWest Country Club for an ace.

He never swung the club again.

Pierce had bought the club—a Tommy Armour 845 6-iron—as part of a replacement set after someone broke into his pickup truck and swiped all his clubs. Though he had been an avid, near-scratch golfer, Pierce was so upset that he didn't bother buying the new set for five months.

"Finally, one day, the guys I worked with pestered me into buying some clubs and then we headed right out to MetroWest to play," Pierce recalled. "We got to the course late so I didn't even have time to hit a practice shot. I was peeling the plastic off the clubs on the first tee."

For someone who hadn't touched a club in five months since the burglary, Pierce was playing well. After 14 holes, he was only five over par, already up "$30 or $40" on the friends who had goaded him into playing.

Then, at the par-3, 168-yard 15th hole, Pierce had

an impending shot that required his 6-iron for the first time. He tore off the plastic, forgetting to remove the adhesive that kept the plastic affixed to the shaft.

"I don't take practice swings, and as I stood over the ball with the club motionless, I noticed the adhesive for the first time," Pierce said. "I thought for a moment about backing away and removing it, but then I thought, 'Nah, just go ahead and hit it.'"

With one swing—his only swing ever with this particular club—Pierce stunned himself and his playing partners by knocking the ball into the cup for an ace. After jumping up and down and giving high-fives to his playing partners, Pierce knew immediately what he would do with his 6-iron.

"I shoved that club right back into the bag and didn't take it out again," he recalled. "After the round, I went to the pro shop and had them order me another 6-iron. This one will never be hit again. It's the perfect club."

Cheapest Ransom Paid to Retrieve a Captive Golf Ball

25-cent can of dog food
Larry Compton, 1969
Seminole Lake Country Club
Largo, Florida

Larry Compton, of Needham, Massachusetts, was playing the 17th hole at Seminole Lake Country Club when his golf ball became involved in a hostage situation.

Compton over-clubbed his tee shot and watched it arch over a fence lining the fairway and into a backyard. When the golfer approached the house, he noticed a very unfriendly dog snarling at him.

Behind the menacing dog was a sign that read, "Your ball will cost you a can of dog food." Compton realized that if he wanted his $1.25 ball back, he would have to pay up. So the next day, on his way to the course, the golfer stopped by a supermarket and picked up a can of dog food for 25 cents. Then he went to the house, asking for his ball. He got it back, after handing over the can to a very enterprising 14-year-old boy.

Most Lost Golf Balls That Fell Out of a Tree at One Time

105 lost golf balls
Olympic Club, 1977
San Francisco, California

A big cypress guarding the eighth green at the Lakeside Course at San Francisco's Olympic Club must have been the most cursed tree on the planet.

In 1977, maintenance men gave three huge branches of the old tree a trimming. The men were stunned when the tree showered them with 105 stray balls that it so unforgivingly had gobbled up.

Most Golf Balls Received by a Baseball Superstar as a Gift

3,000 golf balls
George Brett, 1992
Kansas City Royals

Although Fred Couples is one of the top players in golf today, he loves watching baseball more than his own sport.

His favorite major leaguer is his close friend, George Brett, retired superstar of the Kansas City Royals, who owns a home in Couples's neighborhood in Palm Springs, California. The two often played golf together in the off-season.

When Brett collected his milestone 3,000th hit in 1992, Couples wanted to present his pal with a unique gift. So the golfer boxed up 3,000 Slazenger golf balls and sent them to his baseball buddy, assuming that Brett wouldn't have to buy another ball for the rest of his life.

"His garage should be full," Couples said.

8

Weird Course
Records

Most Hazards That Moo on a Golf Course

80 hazards that moo
Dannebrog Golf Club
Dannebrog, Nebraska

Playing golf at the Dannebrog Golf Club is a mooing experience.

Although there are no sand traps or trees, Dannebrog features sand greens and some beefy hazards—cows. More than 80 bovines are free to graze the fairways and rough of the par-34, nine-hole, 2,620-yard course.

"You have to look out for the cow pies," said Ed Boltz, secretary-treasurer of the golf club. "If your ball lands in one, you're allowed a free drop.

"If the cow is on the fairway, you just have to learn to shoot over him or under him. It's not too often that a ball actually hits a cow.

"Every once in a while, a cow might try to eat a ball. If it does happen, then the golfer gets to hit the ball over again with no penalty. Sometimes, a golfer will find slobber all over his ball because a cow picked it up and spit it out."

Golfers are willing to put up with the cows because the animals keep maintenance costs down by helping fertilize the fairways and "mowing" the grass. Greens fees are only $2 and an annual membership is just $15 ($20 for a family).

The cows come into play because the links are part of pasture land that is leased to the golf club by a farmer for $2.50 a year on the condition that the bovines are free to roam the course. (Wire fences keep them off the sand greens.)

A Winged Foot or Pebble Beach it ain't. But the club does boast more than 90 members and hosts an annual tournament in August, called the Bull Pen

119

Open, which draws over 150 participants from all over the country every year.

The 380 residents of Dannebrog hope the event will grow into a major tournament. But that kind of thinking is probably just cow pie in the sky.

Most Golfers Arrested by Their Playing Partner

3 golfers
New York State Trooper Stan Garrant, 1992
McCann Memorial Golf Course
Poughkeepsie, New York

State Trooper Stan Garrant, a self-proclaimed golfaholic, had just finished his shift and stopped by McCann Memorial Golf Course to get in a quick 18 holes before heading home. At the pro shop, he was directed to join a threesome already on the first tee.

As he approached, Garrant observed some very suspicious activity. One of the men lighted a cigarette, then passed it around to the others, who each proceeded to puff and inhale deeply. The officer knew he was dealing with problem grass—and it wasn't the kind he often encountered in the rough.

Garrant identified himself to the trio as the fourth member of the foursome—and as a law enforcement officer. He then escorted his playing partners into the clubhouse and called the Poughkeepsie police department because the marijuana smoking occurred in its jurisdiction.

With the golfers' arrest, Garrant's anticipated round on the links went up in smoke.

Most Golf Carts Used in Tank Training Exercises on a Golf Course

12 golf carts
Company A, 3rd Battalion,
37th Armor Division, 1988
Custer Hill Golf Course
Fort Riley, Kansas

Golfers didn't know whether to gape in amazement or dive for cover when troops in full combat gear conducted tank training exercises on the fairways and roughs—in golf carts!

In 1988, Major General Leonard Wischart, commander of Fort Riley, was looking for ways to cut training costs on the base. When someone suggested that thousands of dollars could be saved by training potential M1 Abrams tank drivers in golf carts, the commander "tanked him" and ordered it done.

So the 200 troops of Company A, 3rd Battalion, 37th Armor Division headed for Custer Hill—a golf course designed by famed Robert Trent Jones, who never dreamed that his creation would one day be used for tank maneuvers. Neither did the golfers who were on the course playing that day.

The Army paid $289 for rental of a dozen carts and greens fees and then deployed the troops in trees and bushes throughout the course. Bunkers and hazards weren't for playing golf; they were for playing war. Instead of using 32-foot, 60-ton tanks with 105-mm cannons, tank drivers operated four-by-six-foot E-Z-Gos.

"Imagine our surprise when over the rise on a fairway hill we saw golf carts driven by camouflaged soldiers," said golfer Robert Smith. "We were wondering if the golf course was under siege."

Added playing partner Mark Johnson, "We thought we'd help them out by lofting some golf balls in their direction so they could pretend the shots were incoming."

Although the Army took plenty of ribbing for using the golf carts, officials pointed out it would have cost $20,000 more if they had used M1 Abrams. Besides, they added, the drills were useful. Said First Sergeant Leslie Axton, "It's the same as playing in a sandbox with little bitty tanks."

Most Singing Coyotes on a Golf Course

6 singing coyotes
Arizona City Golf Club, 1988
Arizona City, Arizona

Coyotes have a howling good time at the Arizona City Golf Club. They frequently roam the course in the early morning and early evening, serenading golfers and area residents.

Usually, the coyotes sing solo or in a duet. But early one morning in 1988, 80-year-old F. "Boots" LeBouton was walking along the course when he encountered a sixsome of caterwauling coyotes.

"I always see at least one coyote," LeBouton recalled. "On this day, one approached me but ran away when I hit him with my walking stick. He breezed away and ran up on a hill and sang a song. Before I knew it, there were six of them."

When LeBouton turned a deaf ear to their musical yelping, the coyotes surrounded their critic, who realized he needed to head out-of-bounds in a hurry. He lit fire to a newspaper he was carrying, burning it page by page to frighten and distract the coyotes. Then he hustled off to safety, leaving behind a crowded barking lot.

Most Four-Legged Caddies on One Course

2 four-legged caddies
Talamore Golf Course
Pinehurst, North Carolina

Llamas have llightened the lload of llinksmen at the Talamore Golf Course.

When the club first opened in October 1991, the management decided it would get the edge on its competitors by offering golfers a service found nowhere else. It's the world's only course where a player can hire two four-legged caddies—llamas named Billy and Dollie.

"With 32 golf courses in this area, we wanted to get a little identity that the others wouldn't have," said club pro John McDougald. "We're the only course in the world that has llamas. They make great caddies and they have a payload of 400 pounds, so two 50-pound bags of golf clubs are no big deal."

For $400 ($100 a bag), four golfers can rent the two llamas. The pack animals, purchased from a breeder in Vermont, are equipped with special saddles that allow golfers to walk the course while the four-legged caddies each carry two golf bags. A handler leads the llamas and draws clubs for the players.

When nature calls for Billie and Dollie, they are respectful of the course, taking care to handle their private business in the rough. And they also are respectful of the golfers and their shots.

"They give a little grunt on good shots," McDougald said. "But if it's a bad shot, they don't say a word."

Not only are the furry caddies a first, but so is the course's unique Rule Number 4: "Golf carts yield right of way to llamas."

Longest Average Time to Play an 18th Hole

60 minutes
Mt. Dundas Country Club
Mt. Dundas, Greenland

The 18th hole at Mt. Dundas Country Club takes an average of an hour to play—assuming you have mountain-climbing gear. Otherwise, you can't reach it at all.

The hole sits atop Mt. Dundas, a 720-foot peak in Greenland, 700 miles north of the Arctic Circle and only 800 miles from the North Pole. Nearby is Thule Air Force Base, where every July 4 the U.S. airmen compete in the annual Dundas Open.

Mt. Dundas is a tortuous course where the rough and fairways are strewn with rocks and the "greens" are 10-foot-in-diameter circles filled with sand.

It's a nine-hole, par-36 layout with no sand bunkers or water hazards—just the result of centuries of sliding glaciers. Crevices, knolls, pebbles, and boulders make for imposing obstacles, and the fairways are adjacent to slopes that drop off treacherously, seemingly to nowhere.

In the Dundas Open, each player carries a square

of carpet from which he hits his shots. He completes a hole by stopping his ball on the sand green, which is rimmed by rocks. He has just one golf club and two balls. If he loses both balls in one of the crevices or cliffs, then he's disqualified.

It's golf at its crudest, most elementary state—particularly on the brutal closing hole, which takes about an hour to play.

The approach shot must carry to the top of a plateau. Then, to reach your ball, you must use mountain-climbing gear to scale a difficult 60-degree incline. "In the Dundas Open," said one competitor, "just getting to the green is a major challenge. Golfing is the easy part."

Most Yards That a Green Moves Back and Forth

100 yards
14th green
Coeur d'Alene Resort Golf Course
Coeur d'Alene, Idaho

One of the most amazing greens on earth, the par-3 14th hole at Coeur d'Alene Resort Golf Course is a floating island that can be moved to within 75 yards of the tee or be shoved back as far as 175 yards away.

Course owner Duane Hagadone got the idea for the floating green when he observed a cluster of logs floating in the lake near a sawmill. So he had golf architect Scott Miller design it. A naval engineering firm drew up the blueprints and a shipbuilder constructed the green in sections, assembled it on the lakefront, and towed it into place.

The 15,000-square-foot, state-of-the-art green,

which cost $1 million, rests on concrete honeycombs filled with buoyant foam topped with a layer of Styrofoam and 18 inches of greensmix. It can be moved forward or backward on a one-inch cable powered by electric winches. Because it weighs 7,500 tons, the green won't bob even in rough water as a golfer is lining up a delicate putt.

The green has two bunkers, one in front and one in back, and a large bank of flowers and conifers in the rear.

At the tee box, a computerized digital display tells the golfers the exact distance to the pin. After they hit their tee shots, they board a custom-built ferry to take them to and from the island.

Duane Hagadone said part of the reason he had the moveable floating island built was for its promotional value. Said Hagadone, "Hey, when you're out in this part of the country trying to attract attention, you've got have some 'sizzle.' "

9

Outlandish
Putting Records

Longest Time a Golfer Had to Wait to Putt Because the Flagstick Was Stuck in Its Hole

25 minutes
Kim Saka, 1980
Women's Kemper Open Qualifier

Golfer Kim Saka could have used an extra club—like a sledgehammer—to finish the final hole of the 1980 Women's Kemper Open Qualifier. For some mysterious reason, the flagstick was stuck and wouldn't come out of the hole, forcing Saka to wait a frustrating 25 minutes before a groundskeeper finally freed it.

Saka, an amateur golfer from Mesa Verde, California, needed to sink an 18-inch putt for par on the 18th hole to earn the last qualifying spot. Although it was a short putt, she felt the pressure building inside her. With sweaty palms, Saka lined up her ball. But her concentration was broken when she saw her caddie struggling with the flagstick.

Try as he might, the pin would not come out of the cup. He yanked and twisted and wrenched at it, but the rod was firmly grounded. Other caddies took their turn but they couldn't get it out either.

Meanwhile, Saka stood by helplessly, wondering if she would ever get to make the most important putt of her young golfing career. She knew she couldn't hole out while the offending pole was still in place. The Rules of Golf forbid a putt to drop into the hole while the flagstick is in the cup.

Eventually, a groundskeeper was called in to help. With a hammer and screwdriver, he finally ripped the flagstick out of the hole to the cheers of the golfers and caddies. Although shaken by the ordeal, Saka calmed herself long enough to stroke the ball into the empty cup and qualify for the tournament.

"That was the longest half hour I have ever spent," she said. "That putt kept getting longer and longer."

Longest Putt Conceded for a "Gimme" in Ryder Cup Competition

4 feet
Jack Nicklaus, 1969
Royal Birkdale Golf Club
Southport, England

In one of the most exciting finishes ever in Ryder Cup competition, it came down to the final putt on the final hole of the final match between Jack Nicklaus and Tony Jacklin.

After Nicklaus made his par putt, Jacklin faced a four-footer that he needed to hole for the British team to salvage a tie. If he missed the pressure putt, the U.S. team would win.

Nicklaus, though, didn't make Jacklin putt it. In a move that stunned fellow teammates and competitors alike, the Golden Bear picked up Jacklin's marker—in effect declaring the putt "good." As a result, the tourney ended in a 16–16 tie, the only deadlock in Ryder Cup history.

Nicklaus was immediately hailed around the world for this extraordinary act of sportsmanship. But not everyone thought it was right. Frank Beard, a member of the American squad, said most of his teammates were upset.

"Oh, we were irate—I was, for sure," Beard wrote in his book *Making the Turn.* "It may have been a great gesture for Jack Nicklaus, but the other eleven of us had worked very hard and we wanted to win. He just arrogantly assumed that the team and the country, individually and together, would want him to make this sporting gesture. . . .

"I've heard people say it was a very short putt, something in the one- or two-foot range. The putt was actually no less than four feet, and my guess at the time was five.

"Looking back, I recognize the conceded putt as the act of a man of considerable class and sophistication. But I guarantee you, if I'd had the same decision to make, Tony Jacklin would have had to show us he could make a four-footer with the weight of a whole nation on his shoulders."

Longest Measured Putt to Save a Quadruple Bogey

127 feet
Floyd Slasor, 1972
Moon Valley Country Club
Phoenix, Arizona

Floyd Slasor, of Phoenix, Arizona, was on Moon Valley's 10th green, 127 feet away from the pin, when he putted the ball firmly in the direction of the flag.

Incredibly, the ball dropped in for what was the longest measured putt at the time. After Slasor finished his round, club members had already heard of the remarkable coast-to-coaster. The golfer politely accepted their congratulations, then felt compelled to make an embarrassing admission.

"It wasn't for a birdie," he told them. "It was for an eight."

Most Consecutive Holes in Which a Golfer Putted One Stroke Less Than the Previous Hole

5 consecutive holes
Willard Moore, 1977
Tides Country Club
St. Petersburg, Florida

Willard Moore of Hopkinsville, Kentucky, was playing the Tides Country Club when he experienced one of the most unusual putting oddities in golf.

Not quite used to the greens when he began his round, Moore four-putted the first hole. He was still struggling on the second green with a three-putt. But he improved on the third hole by two-putting, and he kept alive his streak of putting a stroke better on each successive hole with a one-putt on Number 4.

At the par-3 fifth hole, there was only one thing Moore could possibly do to make one less putt than the previous hole. And that was not to have to putt at all. Incredibly, Moore finished the hole without a putt. After missing the green with his tee shot, he proceeded to chip in on his next swing.

Moore had completed a rare progression of putts—4-3-2-1-0.

Longest Putt Holed After Being Shot with a Pellet Gun

30 feet
Dr. Tom Jones, 1992
New Albany Country Club
New Albany, Indiana

As Dr. Tom Jones was bending over to line up a 30-footer on the 10th green, a shot rang out. Suddenly, the doctor grabbed his rear and yelped in pain.

His posterior, clad in bright red pants, had been too inviting a target for a youngster wielding a pellet gun. The kid and his two accomplices had been lying in ambush on a brush-lined creek bank across from the green, waiting for the right bull's-eye to come along.

Dr. Jones was not a man who stood idly by after his butt had just taken a potshot. He sprinted across the creek, through the thick brush, and collared one of the youngsters. The culprit quickly ratted on the other two and they were all turned over to the New Albany police.

Most golfers would have considered their round finished after such an assault. But not Dr. Jones. He returned to the 10th green, where his partners were still waiting. And so was his 30-footer.

Again, he lined up his putt and, with remarkable nerves and concentration, knocked the ball right into the cup.

Most Putts Stroked with a Worn-Out Hip Joint

2,500 (estimated)
Claude Petrov
St. Louis, Missouri

When amateur Claude Petrov told his fellow golfers that he was the hippest putter around, he meant it.

He played with a unique putter—one made from his worn-out manufactured hip joint.

Shortly after he started playing golf at the age of 65, Petrov needed a hip joint replaced with a synthetic one. But five years later, in 1978, the prosthesis wore out.

This time his doctor decided to replace the man-made joint with a bone graft.

"What are you going to do with the prosthesis?" Claude asked.

"Throw it away," his doctor replied.

"Hold on just a minute," Claude said. "I can do something with it."

The doctor removed the old joint—which included a steel pin 10 inches long—and handed it over to Petrov. While he was recovering, the 70-year-old golfer found someone who could fashion the old joint into a putter.

"Now I'm playing with my new hip, and putting with my old hip—and doing it very well," Petrov reported shortly after the surgery.

Most Time Elapsed Between the Final Two Putts to Win the U.S. Open

12 minutes
Jack Nicklaus
1962 U.S. Open

In all the excitement of winning the 1962 U.S. Open, Jack Nicklaus forgot to hole out.

Nicklaus and Arnold Palmer had been locked in an 18-hole playoff at Oakmont Country Club near Pittsburgh. Palmer, who grew up just 30 miles away in Latrobe, did not have a good day. On the 18th green, he holed out with a 74, three strokes behind Nicklaus, whose ball was just 30 inches from the cup. Realizing victory was virtually impossible, Palmer walked over to Nicklaus' ball and, being the gracious man that he is, picked it up and handed it to Nicklaus, conceding the putt, and, thus, the match.

The gallery raced onto the green, engulfing the two players and caddies, along with the marshals and scorers. Nicklaus and Palmer were being swept toward the scorer's tent when an alert United States Golf Association official noted there was a rules oversight.

In medal play, which the Open is, an opponent cannot concede a putt. Each stroke must be made over the entire 18 holes. Had Nicklaus signed his scorecard with a score of 71, he would have been disqualified for signing an incorrect total.

Joe Dey, the secretary of the USGA, received the news in stunned disbelief, then realized that an error had indeed been committed. He was able to reach Nicklaus before the winner had signed his scorecard and ushered him to the green so the final stroke could be made.

After a lengthy delay, Dey placed Nicklaus's ball at a spot thought to be where Palmer had picked it up. Nicklaus then crouched over the ball, studied the line momentarily, and drained the putt to officially seal his victory.

Longest "Gimme" A President Coerced Out of an Opponent

3 feet
John F. Kennedy, 1962
Seminole Golf Club
North Palm Beach, Florida

President John F. Kennedy was playing golf with his aide Chris Dunphy at storied old Seminole Golf Club when he hit a nice approach shot to within three feet of the pin.

Although Kennedy's shot was outside what most golfers consider an automatic make, the President reached over his ball and, preparing to rake it away with his putter, asked, "That's a gimme, isn't it?"

"No," Dunphy said sternly, refusing to be intimidated by the most powerful man on earth at the time. "That's a character builder."

But JFK wasn't about to attempt that putt. Instead, he tried a little friendly persuasion. Looking at his watch, he said, "We have to hurry to finish this round. I'm having lunch with [IRS Commissioner] Mortimer Caplan. We might end up talking about auditing some of the White House staff."

Dunphy wasted no time. He knocked the President's ball away, saying, "It's good."

10

Silly Mishaps

Most Times Beaned by a Ball Hit by the Same Golfer

2 times
Fred Farris, 1978
Highland Meadows Golf Club
Sylvania, Ohio

Golfer Fred Farris painfully learned that he should never play on the same course as Dick Crandall.

Farris was standing on the 16th fairway at Highland Meadows, waiting to hit to the green, when a ball crashed into his head. The ball hurt him, but fortunately it didn't knock him out. Farris then found out that the ball was struck by Crandall, an apologetic fellow duffer who had mis-hit his drive from the sixth tee.

Four days later, Farris was back at Highland Meadows, nursing a big knot on his head but still able to play golf. While standing on the sixth fairway near where Crandall had hit the drive that beaned him, Farris was again struck by an errant shot, this time flush on the arm. Luckily, he wasn't injured.

Farris was flabbergasted to discover that Crandall was once again the culprit. Incredibly, Crandall had clubbed his wayward shot from the 16th tee near where Farris had been conked the first time.

Said Farris after his second hit in a week, "From now on, I'm checking on Dick's whereabouts every time I play Highland Meadows."

Longest Drive Ever to Strike a Spectator

506 yards
George Bayer, 1948
Las Vegas, Nevada

George Bayer stood 6'5½" tall and was known as one of the longest hitters ever on the PGA Tour.

Playing in a tournament in Las Vegas, Bayer hit a drive that rocketed off the tee. Fans whistled in awe as the ball flew over 400 yards on the fly. The ball bounced once on the green and then plunked a stunned spectator on the shoulder. The gallery was even more impressed because Bayer's long-distance drive hit a fan who was standing about 30 yards behind the flagstick—of a 476-yard hole!

That wasn't the longest shot of Bayer's career, though. Once, playing in Sydney, Australia, Bayer's shot on a 586-yard par-5 was so close to the green that he needed only a short chip to reach it. Ever the modest one, he noted, "I had a following wind."

Most Stitches Needed by a Pro Who Was Injured by a Clam

5 stitches
Mark O'Meara, 1992
Orlando, Florida

Mark O'Meara was knocked out of the World Series of Golf—by a clam!

A week before the event, O'Meara hopped onto his Wave Runner at a lake near his home in Orlando, Florida. As he lurched forward in shallow water, he lost his balance and shoved his hand into the muddy lake bottom in an attempt to right himself.

"I knew something was wrong immediately," O'Meara recalled. "I looked down and there was a clam shell. I had dragged my left hand over it and taken a pretty deep cut." The base of his thumb was sliced open by the clam. The golfer went immediately to a medical clinic where the cut was sterilized and sewn up with five stitches.

O'Meara waited five days before hitting a ball, then went to Akron, Ohio, for the World Series of Golf. He arrived at noon on Wednesday and headed immediately to the golf course where he registered for the event and then walked to the driving range.

"I took out my 6-iron and made a couple of soft, easy swings," he said. "My thumb hurt like hell. Then I really let go with the third swing, hitting it full out. I almost went to my knees, the pain was so bad."

He flipped the club back to his caddie, told officials he couldn't play, and caught a ride to the airport.

"I was back home in time to eat dinner at seven," O'Meara said. "One day of flying a 2,000-mile round-trip to play in a golf tournament, and I didn't even miss dinner."

Most Holes Played While Holding an Ice Bag to One's Head

11 holes
Greg Powers
1982 Greater Erie Charity Classic

Aside from the usual number of clubs in his bag, golfer Greg Powers needed one piece of extra equipment to complete a tournament—an ice bag.

For 11 holes, at the 1982 Greater Erie (Pennsylvania) Charity Classic, Powers walked down the fairway holding an ice bag to the left side of his forehead after knocking himself out in a freak accident.

On the eighth hole of the final round, Powers uncorked a wild tee shot that finally settled behind a tree. Surveying the awkward situation, Powers realized he had virtually no room to follow through on his swing.

One option was to accept his fate and move the ball a club length away, declaring it an unplayable lie with the resulting one-stroke penalty. However, since he did have room for a backswing, Powers decided to go through with the shot, knowing that his club would stop abruptly as soon as he made contact with the ball.

He selected a 3-iron and took a full swing. The ball sailed off, but his club whacked into the tree. The shaft snapped on impact and the clubhead whipped all the way around the trunk, smacking Powers on the left side of the forehead. The blow left the golfer sprawled unconscious on the ground for five minutes. Doctors were summoned and, after an on-site examination, advised him to withdraw from the tournament.

But the plucky Powers refused, reasoning his only injury was a bad headache and some bruised pride. After a marshal gave him an ice bag to help hold down the swelling and to numb the area, Powers continued to play. For the rest of the round, he held the ice bag to his temple until it was time for him to hit. Then he put it down, took the shot, and immediately placed the ice bag back on the injured area.

Ironically, Powers actually played better with the ice bag than he had prior to the mishap. He shot the final 11 holes in three under par, finishing the day with a 65, and a total of 134 for the two-day tournament.

That was good enough for fourth place, but Powers wasn't around to accept any congratulations. As soon as he signed his scorecard after the 18th hole, he was taken to Erie Hospital. There, an examination determined he had suffered a concussion.

Longest Time a Pro Was Locked Out of His Hotel Room in the Nude

45 minutes
Sam Torrance, 1991
Nice, France

Following a round at the 1991 Mediterranean Open in Nice, France, Scottish pro Sam Torrance returned to his hotel late in the afternoon, doffed all his clothes, and lounged outside on the balcony of his room.

What started out as a relaxing respite turned into an embarrassing predicament.

Stretched out in the nude, Torrance let the ocean breezes flow over his body. He was drifting off to sleep when suddenly a gust of wind slammed the door shut. Torrance got up and, with a sickening feeling in his stomach, reached for the handle. As he feared, the door was locked.

For a full 45 minutes, as the sun set and a cool, damp breeze swept in off the ocean, Torrance stood shivering in the buff. He was finally rescued after he hailed a shocked passerby below, told him his tale of woe, and asked him to send up help.

The next day, Torrance exposed himself to further mortification when he shot a pitiful 77.

Most Major Ailments in a Professional Career

9 major ailments
Andy North, 1970–91

Some people remember Andy North as the man who won two major tournaments in his career—the U.S. Open in 1978 and 1985.

Others know him, though, as the walking operating room. When it comes to health, Andy North's has continually gone south. Here's a list of the major ailments he's suffered:

- 1970: Left knee surgery
- 1983: Bone spur removed, right elbow
- 1986: Broken thumb
- 1987: Arthroscopic surgery, both knees
- 1988: Arthroscopic surgery, left knee
- 1989: Bone spur removed, neck
- 1989: Injured shoulder
- 1990: Arthroscopic surgery, left knee
- 1991: Four surgeries to remove skin cancer from nose and left cheek; plastic surgery to rebuild nose

Not included in the casualty list is a chronic bad back. "If I hadn't played when I was hurt," he said, "I wouldn't have teed it up in the last 20 years.

"It's become a joke in the locker room. Guys don't ask me, 'How was your winter?' They ask me, 'What kind of surgery did you have this past winter?' "

Ironically, it was an unusual ailment that first led North to golf. When he was in the seventh grade, a bone in his knee stopped growing and began disintegrating. North ended up on crutches for 18 months while his knee was repaired. Because he couldn't play his favorite sports of basketball and football, he took up golf. He became a star linksman in high school and college before turning pro.

Battered and bruised, North still tries to play. That is, when he isn't recovering from yet another surgery.

"Right now, I still spend two hours a day on rehab, every single day," he said. "Since 1985, all I've done is rehab."

Most Stitches Required After Strangling a Golf Club

6 stitches
Wayne Levi
1977 U.S. Open qualifier

Pro golfer Wayne Levi tried to choke his driver—and it retaliated!

At the U.S. Open qualifier in 1977, Levi needed only to finish with two pars on the final two holes to make it into the field for the biggest tournament of the year. On the 17th hole, he whacked a dreadful snap hook that flew out of bounds. Bogey was a certainty; double bogey was a definite possibility.

Levi was so angry that he gripped his hands around the neck of his driver and began to strangle it, shaking it in front of his face. Unfortunately, Levi shook it a little too hard. The shaft flexed and the head of the driver smacked him right in the mouth!

The impact loosened a tooth and cut his lip, and blood immediately began spurting down the front of his shirt. He hurriedly hustled to the scorer's tent where a doctor repaired the damage with six stitches.

The cut that was most important to Levi, though, wasn't the one on his lip. It was the tournament's—and Levi missed it.

Most Miles a Golf Writer Traveled in the Wrong Direction to Cover the Masters

1,070 miles
Bob Warters, 1992
Editor, Today's Golfer

Bob Warters, editor of the British magazine *Today's Golfer*, planned to fly from England to the Augusta National to cover the 1992 Masters. So he called his travel agent to book him on a flight to Augusta.

Everything went well on the first leg of the journey—a flight from Manchester, England, to Boston. After Warters cleared customs at the Boston airport, a friendly airline attendant looked at his ticket and pointed him to a nearby gate.

Warters boarded the plane and was a bit concerned when he noticed it was a prop and not a jet. Props are for short commuter hops. Augusta, Georgia, was more than 1,000 miles away. Oh, well, he thought. That's airline deregulation for you.

But Warters became even more concerned after the plane took off. He looked out his window and noticed something just wasn't right. "The ocean was on my right side, not my left," he said. "I surmised that we were headed north, but I figured it was just some quirk in the traffic pattern, that before long the pilot would turn around and get headed in the right direction."

But then the plane landed. Warters looked at his watch and noticed he had only been in the air for 50 minutes. The flight on a jetliner should have taken two hours. Something definitely wasn't right.

Warters went into the terminal and asked in his British accent, "Is this Augusta, Georgia?"

"No," came the reply. "You're in Augusta, Maine."

Aghast, Warters hustled back to the airline counter. He had to spend the night in Maine plus pay an extra $150 for a new plane ticket. But eventually he made his flight to Augusta, Georgia—in time to cover the Masters.

11

Wacky Money and Prize Records

Highest-Priced Cow Ever Won by a Pro

$5,000
Ian Baker-Finch
1988 Bridgestone/Aso Open

The most "udderly" ridiculous prize that pro Ian Baker-Finch ever won on the golf course was a cow!

The Australian, who joined the PGA Tour in 1990, knew he would receive some sort of bonus in addition to money for finishing first in the 1988 Bridgestone/Aso Open in Japan. He was expecting something like a car or free air travel.

"As I was standing on the 18th green at the end of the tournament, one of the organizers led a cow over to me," Baker-Finch recalled. "Aso is famous for its beef and dairy products, and a local farming cooperative had donated this heifer as a prize."

At first, Baker-Finch didn't know what he was going to do with a cow. "I suppose we could have cut her up right then and had ourselves an Aussie barbecue," he joked.

Instead, the golfer conveniently sold the cow back to the organizers for $5,000.

Biggest Winner's Check a Pro Attempted to Throw into the Fireplace

$45,000
Lanny Wadkins
1977 PGA Championship

When Lanny Wadkins won the 1977 PGA Championship—his first major—at Pebble Beach, he planned to celebrate in a big way. It nearly cost him his entire winnings.

After he collected his winner's check of $45,000 in a grand ceremony and spent an hour in the media room giving interviews, Wadkins returned to his swank hotel room with his wife, Penny.

Their room had been stocked with champagne and beer because the management believed Wadkins would be hosting a victory party. Nestled in front of the fireplace, Lanny and Penny began partying by themselves by having a glass or 10 of the bubbly.

"By the time nine o'clock rolled around, we were out in the street trying to hold each other up," recalled Wadkins. Realizing they were in no condition to go anywhere, the tipsy couple stumbled back into their room and immediately fell into a deep sleep.

"The next thing I remember was waking up around 4:00 A.M. because the room had gotten warm," Lanny said. "I got up and noticed a crumpled wad of paper on the floor. Yes, it was my check for $45,000. At some point during the night, I had tried to throw it into the fireplace. Thank God I missed.

"I carefully smoothed out the check and went back to bed," Wadkins recounted, adding that before falling back to sleep he said a little prayer of thanks for being too tipsy to hit the fire.

Most Prize Winnings Turned Down for Shooting an Ace

$90,000
Yoshiaka Ono
1981 Singapore Open

Seldom in golf history has there ever been a more perplexing dilemma than the one that faced Yoshiaka

Ono after he scored an ace on the 17th hole at the 1981 Singapore Open.

The dilemma? Whether to accept $50,000 in cash and a $40,000 car—the special bonus offered to anyone who made a hole in one on Number 17 during the event held at the Singapore Island Golf Club.

The 25-year-old Ono, who operated his father's electrical contracting business in Japan, was an amateur at the time of the shot. He was rejoicing over his great luck in winning the cash and car when someone reminded Ono that if he accepted the booty, he would become a professional. No longer could he participate in amateur events.

Although most scratch golfers would gladly give up their amateur status in exchange for accepting $90,000 in prize winnings, Ono was different. Cradling his head in his hands, the perplexed golfer sat in the locker room for three hours and tried to make a decision. He played golf for the love of the game and enjoyed competing in amateur events. Was it worth $90,000 in winnings to give that up?

Echoing the thoughts of many of his fellow competitors, a golfer walked over to Ono and declared, "Take it! The hell with being an amateur!"

Finally, Ono stood up and announced, "I don't want to be a professional. . . . But I'll never forget Singapore."

Least Amount of Money Pocketed After Winning a U.S. Open

$0.00
Gary Player
1965 U.S. Open

Gary Player didn't pocket a dime by winning the 1965 U.S. Open in an 18-hole playoff over Ken Nagle at Bellerive Country Club in St. Louis. When it came time to receive the winner's check of $25,000, Player declined to accept it personally, living up to a pledge he had made three years earlier.

In 1962, the South African pro vowed publicly that if he ever won a U.S. Open, he would give all the prize money to charity.

The $25,000 purse—worth over $100,000 by today's standards—represented a sizable increase over previous years, primarily because of golf's newly recognized television revenues. At the ceremony, Player announced that $5,000 would go to cancer research in honor of his father, who had died of the disease. The remaining $20,000 would go to the U.S. Golf Association for the promotion of junior golf.

"I always felt so fortunate to have the opportunity to play golf in the United States that I wanted to give something back to express my gratitude," Player said. "I think the United States has a wonderful program for junior golfers—something I would like to see in my country—and I will do whatever I can to promote it. This was just a small token of my appreciation for being allowed to support my family by playing golf in this country."

Actually, Player lost money by winning the U.S. Open. He gave his caddie $2,000 out of his own pocket, representing the 8 percent of the prize money that caddies normally receive.

Most Money Paid Out in One Day by a Resort to Golfers Who Collected on Their Snow Insurance Policy

$7,100
Sands Oceanfront, 1992
Myrtle Beach, South Carolina

When the Sands Oceanfront took out rain insurance for its golfing guests, the word *snow* was added to the policy as a joke. After all, this was Myrtle Beach, on the Atlantic Ocean, where it's not supposed to snow.

But it was no joke when a surprise two-inch snowfall hit in late January 1992. Forty-eight golfers at the hotel presented management with the paid-up insurance policies. The total tab to the resort was $7,100.

Most Money Won by a College Golfer with One Swing of His Club

$1 million
Jason Bohn, 1992
Harry Pritchett Golf Course
University of Alabama
Tuscaloosa, Alabama

With one swing of his club, University of Alabama golfer Jason Bohn lost his collegiate eligibility and his amateur status. But he didn't mind. That's because he pocketed a cool $1 million by sinking an ace.

Bohn, a 19-year-old sophomore chemistry major from Mifflinburg, Pennsylvania, was competing in the 1992 Hole 'N One Shootout—a charity event to raise money for renovation of Tuscaloosa's historic Jemison House mansion. After a preliminary round, each of 12 finalists had a one-shot chance at the million bucks if he could ace the 135-yard second hole at the college's Harry Pritchett Golf Course.

With his 9-iron, Bohn lofted the ball onto the green where it landed to the left of the cup, bounced twice—and rolled right into the hole. And suddenly Bohn—a walk-on hoping to win a scholarship on the golf team—was an instant millionaire. He will pocket an annual check of $50,000 for 20 years.

But there was a price to pay. By accepting the prize money, Bohn had to quit the Crimson Tide golf team because he was now considered a professional. "I was looking forward to playing," he said. "I think I'm going to really miss being on the team. But it didn't take me long to decide what I was going to do. This is a once-in-a-lifetime opportunity."

Minutes after nailing his million-dollar ace, Bohn called his father, James, back in Mifflinburg and told him, "I have some good news and some bad news. The bad news is I'm no longer on the golf team. The good news is I'm now the fourth highest money winner on the PGA Tour."

Most Money Won by a Pro Thanks to a Phone Call

$7,733
Bob Goalby, 1970
Las Vegas, Nevada

Bob Goalby had a fitful time at the 1970 Sahara Invitational, struggling along on an easy course to shoot 71-75 in the first two rounds. Fully expecting to miss the cut because of such mediocre scores, Goalby walked into the locker room, packed his bags, and headed to the airport.

Eventually he heard the boarding call and got on the plane. But while sitting in his seat waiting to pull away from the gate, he began thinking. He looked out the window and saw the wind had picked up considerably. Then he remembered how bumpy the greens had been that day. Maybe, just maybe, the scores are going to be higher than I anticipated, he thought.

Goalby hustled off the plane and ran to a pay phone. To his surprise, he learned he had made the cut.

Given a reprieve, Goalby frantically retrieved his clubs and luggage and caught a cab back to the hotel. Instead of moping at home over the next two days, he played in the tournament. And as luck would have it, he caught a hot streak, shooting a pair of 66s in the final two rounds.

As a result, Goalby finished in a tie for second and was presented with a check for $7,733—money earned thanks to a last-second, 10-cent phone call.

Most Years a Tour Pro Was Sponsored by a Band Leader

3 years
Gary McCord, 1974–77

When Gary McCord graduated from Qualifying School, he quickly realized two facts: he couldn't afford to support himself on the Tour, but he knew a very wealthy neighbor who could.

Famed band leader Lawrence Welk lived down the block from McCord's family in Escondido, California. There was one problem, however. McCord had never actually met Welk. But that didn't stop him from placing a telephone call to Welk's business agent, just in case there might be interest.

McCord was delighted a few weeks later when he received a call from Welk, who offered a proposal: Welk would sponsor McCord for three years. In return, McCord would represent Welk's Country Club Village, a mobile home park with an 18-hole, par-3 golf course. McCord readily agreed.

A month later, at Welk's invitation, McCord appeared on the band leader's TV show. To the young golfer's surprise, Welk asked McCord to hit a ball at an archery target 35 feet away. Shaking like a leaf— and praying he wouldn't embarrass himself—McCord wowed the audience when he hit the target with a 4-iron.

Shortest Time to Win a New Truck in a Golf Tournament

10 seconds
Bob Heath, 1992
Deercroft Golf & Country Club
Wagram, North Carolina

At a charity fund-raiser at Deercroft, a new GMC truck was being offered to the first person to make an ace on the 12th hole. It was a shotgun-start tournament, meaning foursomes would start on all 18 holes at once. Bob Heath began the tournament at Number 12.

He was playing for the first time with a new set of Ping irons. He removed the plastic from his 7-iron, stepped up to the ball, and swatted it. It flew in for a hole in one, and Heath drove home with his new set of irons in a brand-new truck.

Most Money Paid for a Round That Could Have Been Free

$40
Scott Gaertner, 1992
Stonecreek, The Golf Club
Paradise Valley, Arizona

Stonecreek, The Golf Club tried a promotion to increase business during the slow summer months. It tried to lure golfers with an offer they absolutely couldn't refuse—a round that would cost whatever they felt like paying!

Taking advantage of the one-day-only promotion were 138 golfers, including 34 who had never played Stonecreek before. When each golfer finished the round, which normally cost $20, he chose how much to pay and filled out an evaluation sheet of the course.

Scott Gaertner, a Scottsdale resident, paid $40 for the greens fee, the most of any golfer that day. He said his experience was well worth the money because "the course was in the best shape I've ever seen."

One golfer paid nothing, but that was no reflection on the course. He said he thought his round was worth $25, but because it was his 50th birthday, he treated himself to a day of free golf.

Surprisingly, the promotion may have backfired. The average amount paid for greens fees was $16.12, nearly $4 less than the normal summer weekday rate. Attendance of 138 golfers was down from the normal total on summer Mondays of 192. "When we tell people what to pay, we get more players than when we allow them to pay whatever they want," said Stonecreek marketing director Mike Petty.

Most Cadillacs Won by an Amateur Golfer in the Same Event

2 Cadillacs
Ross Applegate, 1976–77
Del Webb Sahara Tahoe Tournament

Days before playing in the 1976 Del Webb Sahara Tahoe Tournament, real estate salesman Ross Applegate, of San Jose, California, bought a Cadillac, which he and his wife, Patricia, drove to the event.

He could have saved the money he spent on the car.

Playing the Incline Village Golf Course's par-3 15th hole, which featured a closest-to-the-hole prize, Applegate swung his 8-iron and left his shot just 23 inches away from the cup. It was the hole's best tee shot of the day, so Applegate was given the keys to a new Cadillac.

Since his "old" one still seemed to be running just fine after three days out of the showroom, Applegate sold the car he had just won. He went home with $9,500 instead of the Cadillac.

A year later, Applegate returned for the same event. Again he won the closest-to-the-pin hole, cozying his tee shot to within three feet of Edgewood Tahoe's seventh hole. The prize was another new Cadillac.

Nope, he told tourney officials, he still didn't need a new Caddy. So he sold the car to the sponsoring casino and walked away with $8,400 in cash.

Most Fattening Endorsement Contract Signed by a Pro

500 Whoppers
Howard Twitty, 1977

PGA Tour pro Howard Twitty is a very big guy, standing 6'5" tall. And he loves hamburgers—so much so that in 1977 he negotiated a small contract with Burger King to display its logo on his bag.

Because Twitty was 51st on the PGA money list at the time, it was an extremely small transaction. Forget the money, he told Burger King. The deal he finally settled on was for 500 free Whoppers. Presumably, they weren't all consumed at one sitting.

Most Bonus Money Missed Out on After Making Two Aces

$20,000
Trevor McDonald
1991 Victorian Open

Golfers at the Victorian Open in Melbourne, Australia, had a chance to win a $20,000 bonus for making a certain hole in one.

Australian teaching pro Trevor McDonald astounded fellow competitors and the gallery by nailing two holes in one in the opening round. He drilled one ace at the fifth hole and the other at the 17th.

Unfortunately for McDonald, he didn't collect one cent of the $20,000. The bonus money was only for someone who aced the *11th* hole.

12

Outrageous Miscellaneous Records

Most Consecutive Holes a Pro Coughed During His Opponents' Swings

17 holes
Seve Ballesteros
1991 Ryder Cup

Seve Ballesteros had a bad case of "sandpaper throat" that rubbed his opponents the wrong way.

Ballesteros and Jose Maria Olazabal teamed up in the opening match of the 1991 Ryder Cup against Americans Paul Azinger and Chip Beck at Kiawah Island, South Carolina. Azinger and Beck were three-up at the nine-hole turn, but the Spaniards won five of the next eight holes to close out the Yanks after the 17th.

Azinger blamed the loss on a distracting habit of Ballesteros's—a constant clearing of his throat whenever the Americans were about to hit. "Believe me, guys, he [Ballesteros] is the king of gamesmanship," Azinger told the press after the match. "He knows every trick in the book."

"That's ridiculous," said Ballesteros. "I just had a bad cold acting up in the chilly ocean air."

The next morning, Ballesteros and Olazabal were scheduled to play Fred Couples and crusty veteran Raymond Floyd. Just as Couples was about to hit his tee shot on the first hole, Ballesteros's cold acted up again, and he loudly cleared his throat.

Floyd walked directly up to Ballesteros, put his nose an inch from Ballesteros's face, and glared at him eyeball to eyeball. Not a word was exchanged, nor was there need for one. Incredibly, Ballesteros's cold didn't bother him the rest of the day. By the way, the Spanish "hacker" and his partner still managed to beat Floyd and Couples 3 and 2.

Strangest Slice Ever Displayed in a Major Tournament

A slice of pizza
Lori Garbacz
1991 U.S. Women's Open

On the 13th tee of the U.S. Women's Open, Lori Garbacz was irked by the slow play of the foursomes in front of her, who were trudging along at a turtlelike pace. So she sent her caddie to a nearby pay phone to order a large pizza to be delivered to the 17th tee.

Sure enough, when she arrived at the 17th tee, the pizza was there waiting for her. So Garbacz ate a slice and shared the pizza with her playing partners, as well as with the group ahead of them—who were still waiting to tee off.

Youngest Fan to Interrupt the British Open by Running Nude on the Fairway

16 years old
Unidentified streaker, 1991

During the opening round of the British Open, a 16-year-old blonde in the gallery tore off all her clothes. Then she ducked under the ropes, sprinted down the fairway, and caught up with Jose Maria Olazabal on the first green. The young Spaniard tried to avoid her, but the streaker managed to throw her arms around the stunned golfer and give him a hug.

After admitting he had lost his composure, a shaken Olazabal said afterward, "By the time I got to my ball, I was OK." Then, trying to act cool, he added, "It was just a naked woman, that's all."

Surprisingly, the young woman was accompanied to the tournament by her mother, who told reporters that her daughter had "always had a mind of her own." The teenager, whom police refused to name because she was a minor, was corralled by marshals who quickly led her off the green. She asked one of the officials for his R&A sweater to cover up with, but he declined. However, a man came down from the grandstand and gave her his raincoat.

Said Nick Price, who was playing with Olazabal, "I've never been so shocked in my life."

Most Unusual Burial Place for a Golfer

The 17th hole
William K. Garner, 1967
Croham Hurst Golf Club
England

William K. Garner was a golf fanatic who lived to play the game. He always said that when he died, he wanted to spend eternity on the links.

He passed away in 1967 at the age of 75. So, according to his wishes, his friends took his ashes to the Croham Hurst Golf Club. There his fellow club members followed out his wishes, but with one final little prank of their own. They scattered his ashes over the area of the 17th hole where he had spent most of his time—130 yards out and in the rough!

Oldest Woman to Play on the LPGA Tour

400 years old (approximately)
Muffin Spencer-Devlin

Pro golfer Muffin Spencer-Devlin, a firm believer in reincarnation, says that in an earlier life she was a 16th-century Japanese woman.

"I know that's true," she said. "The first time I went over to Japan, I had that déjà vu feeling. I'd been there before. The rains, the mists, the temples—everything seemed so familiar."

Spencer-Devlin was so moved by the experience that she immersed herself in the Japanese culture. She attended a language school to study Japanese and now speaks it fluently.

Spencer-Devlin competes in 10 tournaments a year in Japan, where she also regularly appears on TV talk shows. Her command of Japanese made her a natural for providing the Japanese translation on teacher Bob Toski's TV golf show, filmed in the country for Japanese audiences.

Not surprisingly, her best friend on the LPGA Tour is Ayako Okamoto, the most popular female athlete in Japan.

First Reference to Golf as a Health Benefit

1772
Sermons to Gentlemen About Temperance
and Exercise
University of Notre Dame Library

In a 1772 book entitled *Sermons to Gentlemen About Temperance and Exercise* is the first known published remark about the sport's health benefits: "Man would live 10 years longer for using this exercise once or twice a week."

The book was written by Dr. Benjamin Bush, a Philadelphian who had studied medicine at the University of Edinburgh and been exposed to golf in Scotland.

Most Times a Pro Golfer Signed His Autograph with a Jockey's Name

12 times
Bob Toski, 1985

Although he's one of the world's most famous golf instructors, former pro Bob Toski knew that he could never attract fans the way his good friend Arnold Palmer does.

169

Never in the history of the sport has a golfer been so besieged for his autograph as has Palmer. One day, after Palmer and Toski were leaving a country club, autograph seekers surrounded Arnie. As always, Palmer patiently signed each piece of paper thrust in front of him.

In the midst of his frantic scribbling, Palmer noticed Toski being shoved to the side. Ever the considerate friend, Palmer turned to his fans and said, "Get his too."

A curious young man turned to Toski and asked, "Who are you?" Without a moment's hesitation, the slightly built Toski deadpanned, "I'm Eddie Arcaro, the jockey."

At that moment, Toski too was swamped with autograph requests. And he stood there signing the name of the famous jockey at least a dozen times as

Palmer watched in amusement. Later, Arnie asked, "Why did you do that?"

"Well," said Toski with a grin, "there I stood with the world's greatest golfer. You didn't think I was gonna say I was a golfer too, did you?"

Most Times a Golfer Failed the PGA Tour's Qualifying School

16 times
Mac O'Grady, 1971–82

Mac O'Grady began trying for his Tour card in 1971 and failed Qualifying School a record 16 times before finally making it in 1982—on his 17th try. (From 1975 through 1981, the school was held twice a year.)

It was truly a classic case of perseverance from a man who supported himself as a cook, dishwasher, busboy, caddie, and funeral home worker while trying, year after year, to become a pro on the Tour.

O'Grady credited his tenacity and endurance to the stabilizing influence of his Japanese wife, Fumiko, and to the late Homer Kelley, author of *The Golfing Machine*.

"Mr. Kelley told me that the more you struggle with your game, the better player you will become," O'Grady said. "It's good for the heart and the soul to become successful if you've had to face very long odds. The history of the game shows that those who finally survive—the Gary Players, Arnold Palmers, Lee Trevinos, and Calvin Peetes—develop into great players."

O'Grady never developed into a great player. However, he did win $1,013,025 before injuries ended his career in 1990.

Most Tour Golfers Related to Abraham Lincoln

2 Tour golfers
Lon Hinkle and Emlyn Aubrey

Two members of the PGA Tour can trace their family tree to Abraham Lincoln. Honest!

Lon Hinkle is a fifth cousin once removed from the nation's 16th president according to a genealogy commissioned by Lon's great-grandmother, Laurilla Post Hufstader. The tie is close enough that Lon's mother, Nancy Hanks Hufstader, was named for Lincoln's mother, whose maiden name was Hanks.

The other Tour pro who claims a blood tie to Lincoln is Emlyn Aubrey. His connection is a bit easier to establish—his mother's maiden name is Judith Lincoln.

Most Holes Played with a President on a Golfer's Wedding Day

18 holes
Reg Murphy, 1991
Caves Valley Golf Club
Owings Mills, Maryland

Reg Murphy, a United States Golf Association vice president, had a dilemma. President George Bush had just invited him to play golf—but it happened to be on the same day that Murphy was getting married.

What did he do? He played golf—and then got married.

In early 1991, President Bush called Murphy and said, "I've heard a lot of great things about Caves Valley. I'd like to play with you."

Murphy, of course, was delighted and replied, "Any time."

"I'd like to bring along a couple of golfers named Arnold Palmer and [former Attorney General] Griffin Bell," said Bush. "And I have this date in mind—April 25."

Murphy gulped once, then gulped again and told him, "Well, Mr. President, there's a wedding that day." He didn't mention that it was his own.

Bush, though, really wanted to play April 25. "What time is the wedding?" he asked.

"In the evening," Murphy replied.

"We could play early," said the President.

"I guess we're on," said Murphy, wondering how his bride-to-be, Diana, would take the news that he had a golf date on their wedding day.

When she found out her future husband would be playing with the President of the United States, she didn't quibble. In fact, she thought it was great. So Murphy played 18 holes with his famous playing partners and then hustled off to get hitched.

"It worked out fine," recalled Murphy. "I guess that's as good a bachelor party as you can have."

13

Appendix

Do you have any suggestions for new entries that belong in *The Golf Nut's Book of Amazing Feats and Records*?

If you have information about a record that tops any that we have in this book or about a nutty achievement that we neglected to include, please let us know. Here's your opportunity to pay a lighthearted tribute to a game we all love.

Please describe the record in detail. Those that are documented with the best sources, such as firsthand accounts or newspaper or magazine clippings, have the best chance of being included in a future nutty record book.

All submitted material becomes the property of Nash & Zullo Productions, Inc., and will not be returned. Mail your new records to:

Nutty Golf Records
P.O. Box 31867
Palm Beach Gardens, FL 33420